D0122083

WALKING NATURE HOME

Book Twenty
LOUANN ATKINS TEMPLE WOMEN & CULTURE SERIES
Books about women and families, and their changing role in society

A LIFE'S JOURNEY | *Walking Nature Home*

Susan J. Tweit

Illustrated by Sherrie York

UNIVERSITY OF TEXAS PRESS
Austin

The Louann Atkins Temple Women & Culture Series is supported by Allison, Doug, Taylor, and Andy Bacon; Margaret, Lawrence, Will, John, and Annie Temple; Larry Temple; the Temple-Inland Foundation; and the National Endowment for the Humanities.

Appreciation goes to the publications in which the pieces listed below first appeared, before finding their way into this story in different versions: "Walking Home," in *A Road of Her Own* (Fulcrum Publishing, 2002) and *Risk, Courage, and Women* (University of North Texas Press, 2007); "Walking into Love," in the *Denver Post* "Perspective" section (December 5, 2004); "Picking Up Roadkill," in the *Denver Post* "Perspective" section (August 20, 2000), *Earthlight* (Summer 2000), *Pilgrimage* (Spring 2004), and *Earthlight: Spiritual Wisdom for an Ecological Age* (Earthlight, 2007); "The Pleiades," in *The Search for a Common Language* (Utah State University Press, 2005); "Leo," in *Writing Nature* (Summer 2002); "Final Journey across the Sky," in the Salida (Colo.) *Mountain Mail* (September 22, 2004) and the *Denver Post* "Perspective" section (November 7, 2004); "Restoring a Creek, Restoring Hope," in *Wings* (Spring 2006) and *Pilgrimage* 31, no. 3 (2006); and "Knowing What Love Is," in the Salida *Mountain Mail* (February 14, 2007).

Requests for permission to reproduce material from this work should be sent to:
Permissions
University of Texas Press
P.O. Box 7819
Austin, TX 78713-7819
www.utexas.edu/utpress/about/bpermission.html

∞ The paper used in this book meets the minimum requirements of ANSI/NISO Z39.48-1992 (R1997) (Permanence of Paper).

Library of Congress Cataloging-in-Publication Data
Tweit, Susan J.
Walking nature home : a life's journey / Susan J. Tweit. — 1st ed.
p.   cm. — (Louann Atkins Temple women & culture series; bk. 20)
Includes bibliographical references.
ISBN 978-0-292-71917-0 (cloth : alk. paper)
1. Tweit, Susan J. 2. Mixed connective tissue disease—Patients—United States—Biography.
3. Naturalists—United States—Biography. I. Title.
RD924.5.M58T94 2009
158.1—dc22   2008042275

FOR RICHARD
and the community of the land

But to look at the stars always makes me dream,
as simply as I dream over the black dots of the map
representing towns and villages.

VINCENT VAN GOGH,
IN A LETTER TO HIS BROTHER THEO, JULY 9, 1888

CONTENTS

ACKNOWLEDGMENTS

This book owes something to everyone whose life has ever touched mine. My thanks and blessings to you all!

In particular, thanks to those who have helped me map my life, beginning with five teachers from my high school and college years: Richard Olderman, John Richardson, Phil Robertson, John Yopp, and Don Hall.

From Wyoming, the landscapes of my heart, Joan Donnelly, Judy Siddle, and Anne Neale Young, plus the late Terri Edgar and Mary Soll from Cody; former *High Country News* staff Geoff O'Gara, Kathy Bogan, and Dan Whipple; Jim and Becky Kleyman from Jackson; and from Laramie, Virginia Scharff, Susan Kask, Rosemary Hardin, Linda Stanley, my household, especially Dale M. Doremus, and the late J. David Love—I miss you!

From West Virginia, fiction writer Gail Adams, Shano and Mukara, Morgantown Friends Meeting, and Cynthia Christy.

From Olympia, my friends and colleagues at the Washington Department of Natural Resources, including Blanche Sobottke, Craig Partridge, and Nancy Sprague and Bill Phillips; Terry Winfield McLellan, Robert and Judy Garrigues and the late Pamela Lee; and the Olympia Friends Meeting.

From that magic year in Boulder, Annie Douden, Suzanne MacAulay, Vince Snowberger, and Carrie Williams. From Ames, Lisa Brown, the Ames Friends Meeting, and Jan's yoga group.

From our time in Las Cruces, *La Honcha* Denise Chávez y Daniel Zolinsky, Pam Porter, Ron and Vi Cauthon, Sharon Bode-Hempton and Carl Coker, Thad and Jenny Box, Harold and Barbara Harrison, Tom Huizenga and Valeska Hilbig, David Brower and Catherine Lazorko, Ann and the late Brian Palormo; the Saturday breakfast group, including Katherine Durack, Elena Linthicum, Jean Olson, Susan Shay, and Patricia Wendel; Las Cruces Friends Meeting; and Roberta West, who almost lured us to Silver City.

From Salida—home at last!—thanks to Brenda and Mark Wiard, Bev Gray, Bob Spencer, and Bob and Katy Grether; Jerry Scaveeze and Susan Bethany, Toni Tischer, Charles and Doris Frizell, Harold O'Connor, Merry Cox, CC Barton, and Roberta Smith; Paul Ilecki, Kathie Younghans, and Fred and Jeanne Rasmussen; Haven Stillwater of The Book Haven; Jeff and Margie and the staff at Laughing Ladies Restaurant; Kathy Berg, Sherrie York, Jeff Donlan, and the Art Works board; Todd and Patty and the rest of the window staff at the Salida Post Office; and honorary Salidans Peg Logan and Rolfe Larson, Jeff and Ann Lee, and Grant Pound and Peggy Lawless.

Thanks to the health care professionals who have sustained me, especially Judith Bond, Sylvia Crocker, Patti Whitbeck, Donna and Jeff Cooney, Dr. Denise Leonardi, Dr. Mary Reeves, Dr. Barbara Bode, Sharon Borch, Buddy Frank, and Ginny Kelley.

Blessings to my constellation of writing buddies, especially Susan Albert, Janice Bowers, Eduardo Rey Brummel, John Calderazzo and SueEllen Campbell, Denise Chávez, Alison Deming, Carolyn Duckworth, Susan Ewing, David Groff, Debra Gwartney, Kathryn Haber, Kent Haruf, Laura Hendrie, Linda Hogan, Lynda Hoggan, Parker Huber, Lisa Hutchins, Ken Lamberton, John Lane, David Lee, Barry Lopez, Sandra Lynn, Francine Matthews, Ellen Marie Mettrick, Kathy Moore, Gary Paul Nabhan, Christina Nealson, Lisa Dale Norton, Margy O'Brien, Linda Peterson, Laura Pritchett, Bob Pyle, Sarah Rabkin, Deb Robson, Sharman Apt Russell, Primus St. John, Susan Shay, Ursula Shepherd, Steve Trimble, Rosemerry Wahtola Trommer, Terry Tempest Williams, Gary Wockner, Elizabeth Wolf, Ann Zwinger, and that wrangler-of-writers, Mary Lee Adler.

Special appreciation to Peter Barnes and the Mesa Refuge for the gift of time to write, and to my "refuge-mates," Betsy Leondar-Wright and Peter Thomson, for their company.

Thanks to my mentors in publishing, especially Jenny McDonald, Rick Rinehart, Clifford Burke, Mary Ransome, Marlene Blessing, Karen Silver, John Murray, Betsy Marston, Paul Larmer, Jodi Peterson, Mary-Powel Thomas, Rene Ebersole, Jennifer Bogo, Patti Hartmann, Greg McNamee, Jenny Barry, and Jim Steinberg.

My deepest appreciation to Theresa May and the staff at University of Texas Press, including Casey Kittrell, Megan Giller, Lynne Chapman, Nancy Bryan, and Ellen McKie, as well as to freelance copy editor Rosemary Wetherold. Any errors are my fault, not theirs! Also to Sherrie York for the glorious illustrations. And to Susan Brushaber of Schuchat, Herzog & Brenman in Denver, whose advice on book contracts is invaluable.

Blessings and hugs to my family: Molly Cabe, Bob and Joan Tweit, Bill Tweit and Lucy Winter, Heather, Duane and Connor Roland, Sienna, Fiona and Matt Bryant, Alice Joan Tweit, Miss Alice and the late Raymond Cabe, Ron and Bonnie Cabe, Letitia Hitz, Mike and Tami Cabe, Jennifer Cabe and Paul Childress, Andrew and Jenny Cabe, Matt and Shea Cabe, Carolyn and Doug Myrick, and my *antepasados* all.

Last, but most definitely not least, Richard Cabe—bless you, my love.

WALKING NATURE HOME

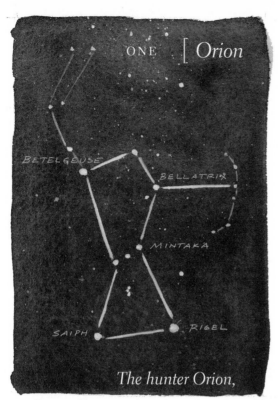

BETELGEUSE
BELLATRIX
MINTAKA
SAIPH
RIGEL

The hunter Orion,

a tall constellation with an hourglass-shaped outline and brilliant stars, strides across the night sky of the Northern Hemisphere from October through March, followed by Canis Major and Canis Minor, his two dogs. Orion rises sideways: his left shoulder, marked by the yellow double star Bellatrix, appears over the eastern horizon first, followed by the brilliant blue-white star Rigel, the seventh-brightest star in the night sky. The three white stars of Orion's slanting belt come into view next. Between the stars marking Orion's dagger, suspended from the hunter's belt, lies the most distant space object visible with the naked eye, the hazy smudge of the Orion Nebula, fifty light-years away. This spangled cloud of gas and shimmering dust is a place of creation: here hot, new stars are born.

"YOU'VE GOT TWO YEARS, or perhaps five," said the doctor, leaning over her metal desk. "I'm sorry."

She took off her glasses and rubbed her eyes, then replaced the lenses carefully before explaining that she had sent my test results to specialists. They concurred with her diagnosis: the way the disease was progressing, they thought, my life would not last long.

It was February of 1980. I was twenty-three years old, attending graduate school while working for the U.S. Forest Service, married to my college sweetheart, and at the beginning of what seemed like a promising career.

I shifted on the slippery vinyl seat of the chair, picked up my mechanical pencil, and recorded her words in tidy script in a ruled notebook. I wanted to remember the facts, so I took notes. I am a scientist. I observe and record from a careful distance. It's what we do, how we make sense of the world.

Just a few weeks before, I had stood breathless atop a narrow ridge hundreds of feet above the Shoshone River, my ski tips aimed precisely perpendicular to the edge. It had snowed all night, laying down a thick blanket of fresh powder. My husband, Kent, and I had risen before dawn, thrown our gear into the truck, and driven the slick and winding highway as fast as we dared. The air was still. The sun threw dazzling sparks from the untracked surface of the snow. My stomach clenched as I surveyed the dizzying drop.

"Go!" said Kent from behind me.

I took a deep breath, flashed a smile over my shoulder, leaned forward, and plunged into an explosion of powder. Hours later, snow-crusted and sweaty from repeating the climb to the top of the ridge and the exhilarating ride down, I hauled myself into the truck.

If you had asked me, I would have said I was perfectly happy.

But my body knew better. I lived in a chill: my bloodless skin was yellow and jaundiced-looking, my hands thin and pale, my toes, lips, and fingertips so numb they were often barely functional. Fevers woke me in the night, my skin drenched with sweat, my muscles wracked with pain. Mornings brought aching joints that creaked audibly, snapping and popping like Rice Crispies in a bowl of milk. Some days my brisk walk turned into a drunken stagger, or I dropped things I thought I had a firm hold on.

I had never examined or cataloged these various ailments, never even thought of them as ailments. They were simply part of life as me.

Until a month before that terrible prognosis, on a night so cold the snowflakes hissed as they hit the windowpane. I stood in the kitchen of our tiny house in Laramie, Wyoming, drying the dishes. I had just picked up my favorite cup, a thick pottery mug glazed deep midnight blue, the color of the night sky just before absolute darkness overtakes it. I was turning the cup round to dry the inside when suddenly it wasn't in my hands at all. Helpless, I watched it hit the floor and shatter.

I woke later in a fever, my flannel nightshirt soaked with sweat. I rolled carefully out from under the covers so as not to disturb Kent and padded barefoot across the chill wood floor to the living room. I parted the drapes and looked up at the sky. Amidst the dazzle of stars of a Wyoming winter night, I picked out Orion. I stood there, arms wrapped tightly across my thin chest, as the hunter wheeled across the sky.

IN ONE OF MY CLEAREST childhood memories, it is dark and I am lying on the ground in my plaid flannel sleeping bag, looking up at a black sky freckled with a dizzying number of stars. My mother is pointing out the constellations: the large, rectangular ladle-shape of the Big Dipper; then, drawing an imaginary line across the heavens from the two stars at the end of the ladle, the North Star, anchoring the fainter form of the Little Dipper; the sideways "W" of Cassiopeia's chair; the faint, tight cluster of the Pleiades; and the towering figure of Orion, marked by his bright, slanting belt.

I fell asleep that long-ago night hearing her voice telling the stories the stars drew in the sky. Orion, seeming to stride through the heavens with complete confidence, was the one that captured my dreams. Since that night, I've looked to the heavens to orient myself, both literally and metaphorically. Whenever I go outdoors after dark, I turn my gaze upward, checking the view of the stars to gauge the weather, and to remind myself of where I am in the year, since the apparent movements of the stars and planets chart the passing of the seasons, and where I am in physical space, since the view is different from different parts of the globe. Looking at the heavens places me in time and space—and beyond them. Gazing at the stars, I look through heaven's wrinkle: the light I see now represents their past, having traveled many years across space to reach my eyes here on Earth; the light they are emitting now will be visible only in some future, years away.

I and all the other lives on Earth are connected to the stars, held together by gravity, the invisible glue that defines our universe, and bound elementally by a common material: stardust. This atomic grit of interstellar space paints dark clouds on the Milky Way, condenses itself into the swirls of gravity-bound suns and planets, and provides the minerals bonded by the push and pull of electrical charges into the molecules that form our cells. Like stardust and the other materials of life itself, we are in constant motion, changing shape as we pass through our lives and, after the makings of our bodies break down and are recycled, rearranged into other forms of life.

The stars remind me of where I come from and who I am.

I MADE AN APPOINTMENT with a doctor. She quizzed me about my symptoms, looked me over, ordered blood tests, and told me to make an appointment to return several weeks later.

I remember the day of my return as the coldest that winter. The sky was a flat, unyielding gray and the wind bitter, straight out of the Arctic. Normally, I loved the energy of Laramie's unceasing wind; it poured through the streets and alleys fresh from the plains, sweeping the town clean. But that day, it bit into my skin.

I pulled open the doors of the clinic and walked into the warmth inside, wiping away the steam that fogged my glasses. The receptionist sent me directly down the hall to the doctor's office. I stared at a framed poster of Monet's garden in cool blues and greens as I waited, fidgety and uncomfortable.

She entered in a rush, carrying a stack of computer printouts, file folders, and books, and apologizing for being late.

"It's good that you came in to see me. Your test results point to a serious illness."

My mouth dropped open, and she hurried on. "First, your test results." She pulled a wide, green-striped computer printout from under the rest of the papers. "After that, I want to talk about your life—your diet, lifestyle, work, mental attitude, emotions, and their affect on your health. But before we meet again," she extracted a book from the stack and slid it across the desk to me, "I want you to read this."

Wait! I thought. She was moving too fast. I couldn't take in the words. What did she mean, a serious illness? I stared at the book. The title stood out in bold type: *Anatomy of an Illness*.

The doctor explained that it was written by a man who had contracted a connective tissue disease similar to what it appeared I had. His innovative approach to the illness might help me, she thought. Medical science, she continued, did not yet understand these deteriorating diseases, and they were often fatal.

My mind stuck on the words "deteriorating diseases . . . often fatal. . . ." There was a roaring in my ears, and my vision grayed.

I took a deep breath. My eyes cleared. I opened my notebook and began to write.

Connective tissue diseases, she was saying, were a group of diseases placed in the same category because their symptoms were similar, although it wasn't known if the illnesses were actually related. These diverse conditions were named for their most prominent symptoms: deterioration of the collagen or connective tissue, the stuff that cushions our joints and connects muscle to bone, nerve fiber to muscle, and cell to cell, allowing us to feel, think, eat, talk, walk, to make love. The deterioration was thought to be caused by a compromised immune system, which, instead of defending us from outside invaders, seemed to turn on our own cells so that our bodies came unglued from within. Sufferers eventually succumbed to either illness-causing pathogens from outside—pneumonia, for instance—or to the interior devastation as organs failed from the stress of the attack. The causes of the different connective tissue diseases were still unknown, so doctors could only treat the symptoms, not address the underlying issues, whatever they might be.

She pulled a text from the pile on her desk. She flipped the pages and then began reading technical descriptions of various connective tissue diseases.

I let the words flow over me. I listened and wrote, but didn't connect. I nodded, but couldn't comprehend.

I was as numb as I imagine a caterpillar would be when her body begins to melt inside the chrysalis, the self she has always known—skin, antennae, eyes, legs, muscle and nerve fibers, and even that ever-clamoring caterpillar gut—dissolving. Does her life flash across her eyes, the crawling weeks devoted to eating and digesting and eating some more, to avoiding being eaten and growing fat? The sudden urge to draw the fine silken threads from within to wind around her body until she is sealed inside a homespun cocoon? Does she dream of the brief winged existence to come when she will be impelled to mate and then to sniff out just the right plant on which to lay the eggs that will carry her genes into the future?

Like the caterpillar's tissues, the life I had known seemed to dissolve with the doctor's prognosis. Only I had no cocoon to shelter my journey into the future I could neither see nor dream.

FINALLY, THE DOCTOR came to the test results. These, the scientist in me could grasp: they were tangible, concrete. I listened and took careful notes as she explained the purpose of each test, and what the data meant. The five vials of blood that the phlebotomist had coaxed from my small, slippery veins had produced pages of numbers.

The doctor circled four results: my sedimentation rate and white blood cell count, the rheumatoid factor test, and the antinuclear antibody test. It was this last, the ANA, that was damning. This test measures whether the immune system is producing antibodies against the proteins that make up one's own cells. My ANA result was strongly positive, pointing to a connective tissue disease. Only which one was not clear: while the data eliminated some of the diseases in this category, they didn't point to one specific disease out of a group that is sometimes difficult to distinguish. (Diagnosing some connective tissue diseases can involve as much art as science. Unlike, say, breast cancer, where a mammogram reveals lumps and a biopsy the presence or absence of different types of cancer cells, for many connective tissue diseases no single test is conclusive. Doctors rely on checklists, ticking off objective test results and subjective symptoms.) It wasn't uncommon, she said, to be unable to specify these diseases in their early stages. There was even a category for that, and me: undifferentiated connective tissue disease.

She looked at her watch. My time was up.

Holding my gaze, she said, "You are a scientist. Do your research. Keep track of your symptoms; take notes. Notice what is happening when a symptom flares up, what makes you feel worse, when you hurt the most, what makes you feel better. Look for patterns in the data. And call me if you need to talk."

Outside, the wind had scoured away the layer of gray cloud, leaving a brilliant blue sky. Shivering, I pulled on hat and mittens and hunched inside my jacket as if it were a cocoon that could protect me from the bitter wind and the words I'd just heard.

I WAS IN SHOCK. Kent and I had moved to Laramie only weeks before to begin graduate school. I knew no one; friends and family were far away. For years, I had kept a journal, a private place to pour out my feelings. But after that visit to the doctor, I had nothing to say to those pages. I talked, yes, repeating the doctor's words over and over without inflection. I could relay the facts, but I could not feel, and I could not write.

I come from a culture that embraces the analytic approach to life: Step back to give yourself objective distance. Look at the problem logically. Gather information. Analyze what you learn. Consider possible solutions. So I treated my illness as a research project. Research follows an orderly, comfortably rational process; messy and potentially painful emotions are not allowed. The first step is to define the problem, the next, to survey the literature and read what others have discovered. Then, design the project and begin collecting data. I went to the library and looked up connective tissue diseases.

What I learned was as bewildering as it was illuminating. More than seventy illnesses are classified as connective tissue diseases (the group is now known as autoimmune diseases), ranging from obscure ones like Sjögren's syndrome to more familiar illnesses such as rheumatoid arthritis, certain types of diabetes, and multiple sclerosis. Although the various connective tissue diseases affect millions of people—over two million in the United States for rheumatoid arthritis alone—these conditions are often unrecognized or misdiagnosed even by specialists. Many symptoms are qualitative and thus easily missed or dismissed, and symptom clusters change radically over time, some mysteriously vanishing altogether, others suddenly appearing. Different diseases also share symptoms. Sufferers often don't appear ill, making it tempting to label their complaints psychosomatic. No wonder that reaching a diagnosis may require years or decades.

Imagine that your skin gradually shrinks and hardens, as if spun too long on a dryer's high-heat setting. Everyday actions like getting dressed become a struggle. Your grip is feeble and your fingers stiff, making it difficult to grasp a doorknob or drawer pull. When you manage to open a drawer and take out a bra, you fight to pull the garment on and fasten it. This is life with scleroderma, where the connective tissue in your dermis—your skin—deteriorates, causing a loss of elasticity so great that your limbs eventually become immobilized as if confined in permanent casts.

Or suppose that you stand up to give a presentation and your mouth is so dry that you cannot speak. Even after you gulp water, your tongue makes flopping and clicking sounds, like a trout thrashing in a drying pool. The lining of your nose is perforated as if you've been snorting cocaine. Your eyes burn, your vagina is chronically dry. These are effects of Sjögren's syndrome, in which lymphocytes attack the moisture-producing glands of your mucous membranes, leaving the viscous surfaces that normally trap and eject harmful detritus and organisms as parched and useless as dry moats.

Or imagine that you wake in the night, drenched with sweat

and shivering uncontrollably from a fever. Your muscles ache as if you've spent hours in physical labor; your joints swell and turn hot to the touch for no apparent reason; you are plagued by fatigue so profound you can barely function. The disease, like the nighttime fevers, comes and goes: some days you feel fine, other days you struggle just to get out of bed. This is systemic lupus erythematosus, known simply as lupus—"wolf" in Latin, for the characteristic pink facial rash thought to resemble a wolf's bite.

I had the joint inflammation, muscle pains, and flu-like fevers characteristic of lupus, the dry eyes of Sjögren's, and skin thinning that indicated scleroderma. But testing couldn't pinpoint which predominated; hence the label *undifferentiated*. In time, doctors theorized, my illness would "mature" into something more clearly classifiable.

What I had learned was sobering: I might live two years, or five, or as a long shot, ten. No one knew what caused my illness, how to cure it, or even what to call it. Potential courses of treatment involved alleviating the various symptoms with various drugs, although there was no known cure for the disease itself, which would continue to "progress"—surely an ironic use of the term when applied to a continuing downward slide.

I had entered the land that Susan Sontag calls "the kingdom of the sick," a frightening territory where life is measured in doctor visits and blood test results, not birthdays or promotions or the other mileposts of a normal life. Where terms like "progress" really mean "steadily get worse," and death is rarely mentioned, especially not to the patient.

IT'S NOT AS IF death was a stranger. I had seen it in the bodies of wild animals my family sometimes stopped to retrieve: the raccoon we had admired while it was still warm and flexible, the red-tailed hawk my father saved for a researcher friend, the yellow-billed cuckoo with its soft plumage and lolling neck that went into our freezer for a taxidermist. My brother still has that bird on his shelf, stuffed, its glass eyes perennially alert.

I saw death up close when my father brought home two "spare" white mice from the laboratory to assuage my continual pleading for a pet, and one promptly killed its cage mate. I buried the small white-furred and pink-tailed body, wrapped in tissues, in an elaborately decorated shoebox, with a full funeral. By the time the surviving mouse died, both casket and ceremony were considerably simpler.

Death brushed closer when a grade-school acquaintance drowned in the opaque, wave-churned water of Lake Michigan while my friends and I tried fruitlessly to convince a lifeguard that we had seen her go under and not surface again. It squeezed my heart when a high school boyfriend, after enlisting against his parents' wishes, didn't come home from Vietnam, and when my beloved grandfather Milner, my mother's father, died suddenly of an abdominal aneurysm during my junior year in college.

I knew death as a scientist. Biologists talk about life in terms of cycles—the hydrogen cycle, the nitrogen cycle, the carbon cycle. In this tale, death is the master recycler, and these elements, the basic building blocks of life, act as transformers, combining into complex alliances and breaking down into simpler ones over and over again, tumbled on their way by death and decay. I learned how death unravels the complex physical form we call a body, releasing muscle from bone, nerve fiber from muscle, connective tissue from nerve fiber, cells from connective tissue, complex proteins and carbohydrates from cells, simple molecules from these complex ones, and so on, until the organism has dissolved, its matter and energy incorporated into some other form.

I studied wildfires, those vortexes of energy that oxidize life, turning living trees into blackened spars, incinerating animal bodies, and transforming green vistas into moonscapes of ash. I learned that in arid climates where the decay necessary to revitalize soils and sprout new life takes agonizing centuries rather than mere months, the deadly power of fire gives forests and grasslands the gift of renewal, as new lives sprout phoenix-like from the fertilizing ashes of the dead.

But until my physician introduced the words "fatal illness" into the vocabulary describing my life, I didn't understand that death applied to me.

AFTER MY DOCTOR delivered the specialists' prognosis, she paused and scanned my face.

"We don't know how to cure this illness, but we do know that your mental attitude and participation are critical. There are intriguing cases in the literature where patients made a major change in their life, changed careers, for instance, or ended a difficult relationship, and their health improved dramatically."

She cleared her throat.

"How is your husband taking this? He hasn't come in with you lately— Is he supportive? Are you happy in your marriage?"

Kent and I had met in college in a university outings club when I was eighteen and he was twenty. We paired up through mutual interests: we both loved the outdoors and adventure, and both wanted to settle the West. We moved in together and took many of the same classes; we married after I graduated. We worked for the same national forest. On our days off, we tossed dog and gear into our truck and went hiking, backpacking, climbing, cross-country skiing, or floating rivers. Life seemed carefree—until my diagnosis.

My focus turned increasingly inward. Waking up each day in my unpredictable body and adjusting to its shifting symptoms more than sated my thirst for adventure; researching my illness stretched my intellectual curiosity to its limits. At first, Kent listened avidly to my reports. But before long, he turned away. One evening when I returned from the library bursting with new information, he interrupted me in midflow.

"I don't want to hear about it!" He grabbed his coat and hat, called the dog, and stomped out of the house into the winter night.

"You aren't dying!" he yelled as he slammed the door. "You are *not* dying!"

I shut down. I quit discussing my symptoms. I scheduled my doctor appointments for times when he was in class or at work. I passed off my library research under the guise of graduate-school projects.

I've never been a successful liar. "Your face is like an open book," my mother once commented. To my surprise, Kent rarely challenged me. We spoke less. Our conversations were careful, avoiding the deceptions that grew between us.

I am, as Kurt Vonnegut's Mr. Rosewater describes himself, "a very slow realizer." It hadn't occurred to me that the shift in our relationship might be caused by my illness. I was pretending my illness was simply another research project. Kent was apparently also in the denial stage. Maybe, like the monkey that could hear no evil, he thought if he covered his ears, the dire news would go away.

Walking home alone one night after a stint in the stacks, I paused in the darkest part of a park near our house, away from the orange glare of the streetlights and craned my neck to scan the sky, searching for the bright shape of Orion.

No matter the chaos and uncertainty of my days, a look at the night sky and its familiar constellations is comforting. The same star patterns appear night after night and season after season. The shapes that we call constellations are not actually fixed, but the movements of the individual stars happen over millennia at a pace much too slow for us to perceive. Their seeming steadfastness reminds me that the universe is based on rhythms so grand and long lasting that my concerns diminish to become, if not trivial, certainly less urgent by comparison. Measured against the brief span of human lifetimes, the constellations appear eternal as they wheel across the sky with the changing seasons, a reminder that life as a whole continues even as our own existence will not.

Until the sky-glow of the industrial era blanked out much of our view of the night sky, our ancestors used the movements of the stars and planets to mark the passage of time and to steer their lives. The myths attached to the dot-to-dot stellar patterns recount our hopes and fears, our beliefs and dreams about what it is to be human.

For the ancient Egyptians, the hourglass-shaped group of bright stars that I know as Orion was the figure of Osiris, the first king of Egypt and the god of death. In Jewish lore, he was the Biblical hero Samson; for the Arabs, Al Jabbar, the giant; in China, the hunter and warrior Tsan; to the Navajo, First Slender One, who impregnated the spring earth with seeds.

The story I know of Orion comes from Greek myth. He was a son of the sea god Poseidon, a hunter of mythic prowess, and a giant of great beauty who loved and pursued many women—and made one so angry she caused his death. Infuriated by Orion's boast that he could kill any animal on Earth, the goddess Gaia called on Scorpius to teach the hunter a lesson. Just one sting from the little scorpion's tail silenced the boastful giant. Placed in the skies to stride across the heavens followed by his dogs, Orion is forever chased by his fate: Scorpius ascends in the east as Orion sets in the west.

The tales that science tells about the stars, the nebulae where they are born and the black holes where they die, are the stories of the origin of our universe, the celestial birthplace of all known life. Both science and myth carry clues to discerning the beliefs and dreams of the cultures we are born to, the perspectives that shape our species. What we see — or don't see — in the night sky is a reflection of how we view ourselves, a mirror of our culture and times.

In my mind, Orion stands for courage, the grit and strength necessary to move forward even when the way is not clear, and for the vulnerability that makes us human. Spotting Orion striding across the black heavens in the breathtaking cold that winter night, I saw the stellar figure as my talisman.

THE DOCTOR WAS elaborating on her theme. Rather than looking to medicines to treat my illness, she said, I might need to fix my life. "Remember the laughter therapy Cousins used in *Anatomy of an Illness*?"

I nodded.

"We don't know how to make you well," she said. "But we do know it's much more difficult to get well if you're not happy."

I was not ready to shoulder the responsibility for fixing either my young marriage or my life. I could handle an intellectual exercise; I couldn't bear emotional examination. I shook off her words the way a dog shakes off flies and headed back to the safe and tidy world of research.

It was a relief when the semester ended and I could pack up our household to return home to northwest Wyoming and another season of fieldwork. I walked the rugged landscape pursuing my research until I was exhausted, filling my brain with observations, data, speculations, and theories. At home, Kent spent hours slouched in an old orange easy chair in front of the television while I sat at the edge of a mesa that overlooked town, listening to the wind. Or I escaped into novels borrowed from the small town library, searching for happy endings.

When I needed company, I went dancing with Charlie, a sweet southern boy who worked with us in summers. I met Joan and Mary, my best friends from the office, for drinks and dinner.

Kent grew jealous. I belonged to my illness now, not him. Once I came home to find him sobbing on the couch. When I sat next to him, he pulled away.

"Where have you been?" he shouted. "Who are you sleeping with?"

His words bit my heart. I wasn't sleeping with anyone else—then.

Another time, I tiptoed into the dark house, and as I crossed the living room, the hair on my neck raised. I flinched just before a thick ecology text from my shelves struck me in the back of the head. I staggered and caught myself on a chair.

"Oh, my God—I didn't mean it! Suz, are you okay?"

I could just make out Kent's form, too near.

"I love you. I'm sorry. I didn't mean it!"

I pulled myself upright and backed carefully out the screen door. I could still hear his sobs as I started the truck and drove away.

That Labor Day weekend, we went backpacking with friends and an early fall snowstorm moved in. All I remember from those three days is a steady rain of wet, white flakes falling silently, muffling forest and lake and rock, pressing down on the roof of our small tent until I felt like I would suffocate. On the long drive out, even the cab of our pickup truck seemed to have shrunk.

I looked over at Kent and said, "I need space. I think we should separate."

His jaw clenched hard, but he didn't turn his eyes from the gravel road. "You'll be dead first."

I moved out. He attempted suicide. I saw a counselor.

One afternoon, I sat in a wicker chair in her office with my chilled hands wrapped tightly around a mug of hot tea, and agonized about what to do: Kent needed me. My health was going downhill. How could I take care of myself and also take care of him?

She listened until my voice trailed off. "Suppose your illness is giving you permission to follow your heart. If you don't have much longer to live, what does your heart want you to do?"

I took a sip of tea and began to cry. My choices seemed at once so clear and so painful.

"Get a divorce," I said, tasting the bitterness of the tears running down my face. "I can't fix both of us. I've got to choose me."

ON THE DAY OF our divorce hearing, I left work early to dress. (In preparing me for this court appearance, my very proper lawyer had looked disapprovingly over the top of his half glasses at my faded jeans and turtleneck and had suggested that I appear "more feminine, but not flashy." Thus, I had visited Cody's most exclusive dress shop and had spent my carefully hoarded savings on a dress with a demure lace collar and a hem very properly below my knees.) I showered quickly and twisted my long hair neatly atop my head in a Gibson girl bun. Shivering with cold and nervous tension, I pulled on hose, slip, and my dress-for-divorce frock and then checked my image in the tiny mirror in my closet-size apartment bathroom. *Damn!* My skin was tinged a deathly yellow shade. I rummaged in the rusted metal medicine cabinet for the makeup I rarely wore, brushed some pale pink powder across my freckles with shaking hands, and carefully painted my lips a brave shade of red.

Half an hour later, I stood before the judge in a nearly empty courtroom at the Park County Courthouse.

After questioning me about the settlement of our meager property, and our lack of "issue" (children), the judge looked down at me from his seat behind the high desk and asked, "You and your husband attempted reconciliation?"

I nodded.

"You swear that the differences cannot be mended?"

I saw Kent's jaw muscle clench tight and heard his flat voice: *You'll be dead first.*

"Yes, sir."

The judge dismissed me to a bench outside the courtroom while he and the two lawyers conferred. I sat straight-backed for courage, goose-pimpled arms hugging my chest for warmth. After a few minutes, my lawyer summoned me back to hear the judge's proclamation: "Divorce granted without protest."

When the brief proceeding was over, my lawyer gently took my elbow to escort me outside. We walked down the wide courthouse steps and, at the bottom, shook hands.

A wave of loneliness washed over me. I clutched his hand like a life preserver.

He looked down at me, his eyes concerned. "Will you be okay?"

How embarrassing! "Of course," I said, carefully withdrawing my hand.

We exchanged good wishes; he walked away.

I looked up at the blue sky, searching for a glimpse of the stars to point my way on a journey that I had never imagined for myself. I was, in Huck Finn's words, lighting out for new territory. Unlike Huck, however, I had no hankering for adventure. I wished fervently for the sight of Orion, striding confidently across the sky.

I squinted, willing the pinpricks of light to appear overhead, but they remained invisible, obscured by the glare of day.

I wiped my eyes and walked home.

TWO [*Aries*

TRIANGULUM

HAMAL

SHERATAN

Aries, the Ram, is an inconspicuous

constellation with prominent associations—it is named for the
Golden Fleece sought by Jason and the Argonauts and also
for the Greek god of war. Aries is easiest to locate in winter: a
line traced between Betelgeuse in Orion and the east corner
of the great square of Pegasus passes through the brightest of
Aries' five stars, Hamal, whose name means "sheep" in Arabic.
The two stars to the right of Hamal are a binary pair linked
like astronomical Siamese twins by a shared gravitational
field. These twins are named Sharatan, or "sign," because they
once marked the spring equinox point, the spot the sun passes
through at the moment it crosses over the equator, releasing the
Northern Hemisphere from wintertime slumber.

"PUT YOUR HANDS IN HERE," said the doctor, pointing to a porcelain wall sink filled with water.

Puzzled, I walked over and dipped my hands into the sink—then pulled them out immediately, shocked by the icy water temperature.

My doctor had sent me to this specialist to check her diagnosis. He greeted me in a perfunctory manner, sat down, and paged through my chart. Then he walked to the sink, opened a tap, and waited in silence until water had filled the sink before instructing me to immerse my hands.

"Keep your hands in the water until I tell you to remove them."

I gritted my teeth and reimmersed my hands.

He looked at his watch.

The cold bit into my skin. The nerves in my hands screamed with electrical impulses relaying pain to my brain, and then finally, blessedly, went silent. An ache worked its way up the bones in my arms to my shoulders and then into my chest. Goose bumps marched their pimply topography across my skin. My fingers turned yellow, then blue, as the capillaries spasmed, shutting off the blood flow, with its essential cargo of oxygen. Tears leaked from the corners of my eyes.

After what seemed like an eternity, the doctor said, "You can take your hands out now."

He took hold of first one limp hand and then the other, examining my fingertips closely. My fingers were as pale as wax, and about that useless. He tapped the middle knuckle of my right hand with a reflex hammer. Nothing happened. He tapped again, harder. My knuckle hurt faintly, like an echo of distant pain, but my fingers didn't twitch.

He dropped my hands, turned away, and began to write in my chart.

"Your blood tests are inconclusive. I can't see anything wrong with you. I suggest you make an appointment with the psychiatry staff."

I stared at his back, unable to find words to respond.

"You can go now," he said.

I stood up, left the room, walked down the hall, and pulled open the door of the clinic. My hands, beginning to thaw, throbbed. My head ached. I fumbled with my jacket but couldn't manage the zipper. I tried and failed to stuff my rubbery fingers into my mittens and finally forced my hands into my jacket pockets. By the time I reached home, my lips were so numb I couldn't talk.

That night, I shivered through wave after wave of fever. After classes the next day, I called my mother.

MY MOM IS AN ARIES in the language of astrology: she was born at the time of year when the Ram accompanies the sun across the sky. Although the constellation is inconspicuous, its birth sign is associated with the war god's fearless and aggressive behavior. My mom doesn't look like a warrior: she's petite and slender, with a cheerful personality, sparkling eyes, and a big smile. She was born so seriously nearsighted that she was declared legally blind and never learned to drive. She's also completely color-blind, perceiving the world in black and white and shades of gray. But she is not helpless; let something tread on her sense of justice, or someone suggest that she cannot do something, and you'd best get out of her way.

When I entered first grade, Mom headed to school too. Despite her poor vision, she earned a master's degree in library science—cum laude. When she took a job as a school librarian, she rode the bus to work. But she was determined to get around on her own, so she decided to teach herself to ride a bike. She wobbled up and down the alley near our house, picking the gravel out of her knees and palms each time she fell, until she found her balance and felt confident to negotiate the streets.

She loved to swim and was fearless in the water. Having honed her strokes in the snow-fed lakes of the Sierra Nevada, she would plunge right into water so cold it quickly reduced me to a shivering rescue subject. I struggled with buoyancy until she taught me the sidestroke, my only aquatic accomplishment. Then came high school and a requirement that each student pass several semesters of swimming—in which sidestroke was not acceptable—as part of physical education. The temperature of the high school's swimming pool exacerbated my natural lack of body fat and floatation. While others perfected their racing strokes, water ballet, and diving form, I turned blue and floundered in the shallow end with the special ed kids. My swimming teacher called me a faker and threatened to flunk me. My mom called our pediatrician, who wrote a note excusing me from swimming for the rest of high school.

When I finished high school a semester early in order to accompany my parents on their sabbatical to Cambridge, England, my adviser (also my former swimming teacher) informed me that school policy dictated that I couldn't graduate unless I was present at the ceremony. I finally told Mom, who promptly wrote a letter to the principal: Susan, it said in part, would be living in England at the time of the graduation ceremony and thus would not be able to attend, since, as the school knew, England lay across the Atlantic Ocean and Susan was not a strong swimmer. My adviser was livid, but my mother won. I was allowed to graduate.

WHEN I TOLD MY MOM about my visit to the specialist, I could feel her anger through the telephone wires from halfway across the West. I was grown up, though; this one was my fight.

I returned to research, approaching my illness as a project in my specialty of ecology, the science that investigates the interactions between living creatures and their environment. The term "ecology," from the Greek *oikos*, meaning "house," and the suffix *ology*, "the study of," literally means the study of our home, planet Earth. Ecology is sometimes split into two branches: synecology, which parses the workings of whole communities and ecosystems, and autecology, the more intimate study of individual animals or single-species populations. My interest has always been the big picture, but here I took a narrower focus and turned to my own home, my body.

After combing the literature to gather what was known about the disease, I shifted to collecting data: observing my health. I postulated a working hypothesis that my mental and physical well-being could affect the outcome of my illness. Each set of observations would test and refine that hypothesis.

It may seem unnatural to make a research project of one's own

health. But looking at it through the eyes of a scientist was sooth-
ing, allowing me to examine my symptoms and their sometimes-
terrifying progress without being paralyzed by fear. Treating my illness as fodder for research gave me enough distance to get on with
my life. The project has turned out to be my most important work,
engaging my interest long after I left the profession of science and
continually challenging my thinking and knowledge, helping me
understand life and regain my faith in it.

First, I gathered data. I bought a blue spiral notebook and a gray
mechanical pencil. I noted my symptoms in careful, precise hand-
writing, as meticulously as I would take field notes for any other
research: the date, time, location, the weather or indoor conditions,
what I, the subject, was doing, exactly what symptom or symptoms
I observed. My tidy notes tell of waking at night in a feverish sweat,
of knuckles swelling into hot, painful knots, of struggling to force
numb, clumsy fingers to write notes during a lecture, of the chunks
of enamel that occasionally flaked off the surfaces of my teeth, of a
winter month when my symptoms progressed from cough to flu to
walking pneumonia.

The early pages are dry, unemotional, the voice of a detached
scientist: "Just the facts, ma'am." But soon another voice, warmer,
more human, emerges after each observation. These jottings, always
in lowercase and posed as tentative questions, suggest solutions: perhaps a cup of hot milk before bed to ease sleep? soak hands in warm
water with baking soda for the swelling? bring a Thermos of hot tea
to class? That voice came from deep within, drawing on a source of
wisdom the scientist in me had forgotten to hear: my intuition, the
part of the thinking process that mumbles along in the background
of the subconscious, sifting through information in search of connections, links critical to our understanding of what is and can be.

Biology is biased toward logic and reductionism: any problem
is simpler to grasp and describe if it is isolated, reduced to its essential parts. Removing the context and the relationships, however,
can render the problem and any potential solution meaningless or
even harmful. The details are critical to the whole, but the whole,
whether one life, an entire landscape, or a single behavior, really is

much more complicated than just the sum of its parts. Neurologist Oliver Sacks tells a story about the mathematician whose disabling headaches Sacks successfully cured, only the man's ability to do math vanished along with his pain. Sacks realized belatedly that he had treated the headaches as an isolated problem, as if they had no relationship to—or affect on—the whole person.

SOME MONTHS after the visit to the specialist who thought my illness was all in my head, I saw an eye doctor. He peered into my dilated pupils and asked if I had a connective tissue disease. The atrophied capillaries in my pupils, he explained, were diagnostic.

"Your capillaries are also visible in the bed of your nails," he said as he wrote in my chart, "but examining them requires chilling your hands first, something to be avoided as it is often quite painful."

My eyes filled with tears.

"Did I say something wrong?"

"No," I said, swamped by twin sensations of relief and grief at his accidental corroboration of my diagnosis.

The ordeal by ice water was my first, but not last, encounter with a doctor who labeled my illness "psychosomatic," a kind way of saying, "It's all in your head." Of course my illness is psychosomatic: the word comes from the Greek for "mind" (*psyche*) plus "body" (*soma*). The two are inseparable. Anything that affects our body also affects our mind, and vice versa. The connection between psyche and soma doesn't make illness any less real. It simply makes our health more complex and difficult to diagnose—and to truly understand.

Western medicine has a tradition of dismissing as hysterical complaints conditions it cannot explain. As recently as the early twentieth century, menopause, a normal part of the aging process for over half of the world's population, was miscast as a mental problem. Women who complained of extreme hot flashes and other symptoms of routine hormonal changes were sent to institutions. By the middle of the century, medicine had progressed to doping menopausal women with addictive barbiturates or removing their "female organs" altogether, and then to suppressing the symptoms with the hormone replacement therapy now implicated in increased risk of a slew of truly scary conditions, including breast cancer, heart disease, stroke, blood clots, and dementia.

AS MY NOTEBOOK filled with observations, I looked for patterns that would help me understand the nature of my health and my relationship with it. I studied my body and its rhythms, trying to sort out what was "normal" for my system from what was "illness." I began by naming each symptom.

Naming gave me a set of metaphorical pigeonholes within which to place the data I gathered: when the symptom happened, how long it lasted, and any factors that seemed to affect its occurrence and intensity, including diet, ambient temperature and other environmental conditions, physical activity, emotional condition, and stress. With sufficient data, I figured I could grasp the symptom's pattern, its place in the ecosystem of my body. Naming brought other benefits I hadn't imagined. "In ancient cultures," writes Buddhist teacher Jack Kornfield, "shamans learned that to name that which you feared was a practical way to begin to have power over it." A name makes the unknown familiar, the frightening comprehensible. A name also determines the identity and significance of the thing named, its place in the universe. When I woke in the night slick with sweat and shivering with a fever, it was calming to remind myself, "Oh yes, night sweats. I know these, they are a familiar part of my health."

As I recognized each symptom, I began experimenting with how to manage or mitigate it. Despite the advice of various physicians, I shunned the pharmaceuticals offered to "manage" my symptoms. Drugs in general do not love me; their side effects, those unwanted consequences, very often outweigh the benefits. The first time I caught a respiratory flu as a child, for instance, our pediatrician prescribed a standard combination of aspirin and antihistamine. I don't recall the flu at all; I do remember the vivid sensory hallucinations conjured by those very mild drugs. I laid on my bed, wide awake, and watched the walls of my room recede, until I, viewing myself as if from above, was just a tiny figure in an immense space.

The walls began to close in again until my body was trapped in the now-dollhouse-size room. Bricks punched up through my mattress. Voices called to me from out of nowhere. My parents carried me to their bed and cuddled me between them until the drugs passed through my system.

Instead of turning to prescription medications, I worked out accommodations to my symptoms. When a fever woke me at night, for example, I got out of bed and rinsed my face with warm water to cleanse any remaining traces of unsettling dreams. Then I heated a cup of milk and padded outside to look at the night sky. Equally soothed by the warm milk and the view of the stars, I could return to bed and sleep.

Accommodating or adapting rather than attempting to suppress the symptoms preserved my opportunity to pay attention, to listen to what they had to tell me about how this mysterious condition worked, specifically, how it worked in my body. That knowledge, it seemed to me, was my best hope for survival in the face of medicine's lack of understanding of what caused my sudden decline, much less how to arrest or cure it. I instinctively treated what others labeled as a disease not as an affliction, infection, or enemy but as a teacher, a source of wisdom that spoke in a language I might not yet be able to understand, but which I was certain carried crucial lessons I needed to hear.

NOT LONG AFTER MY DIVORCE, I woke in my mother's childhood bedroom in Berkeley, curled in a ball under a midden of blankets. My parents and I were visiting my grandmother Janet, who had lived alone since the sudden death of my grandfather several years before. The house and her affairs had become too much for her, and she had agreed to move to a smaller place near my folks in Tucson. When they asked for help in sorting through her belongings and preparing the Berkeley house for sale, I jumped at the prospect of a vacation from my self-imposed research.

The morning's fog had given way to fitful sun, and I could hear my mom and dad talking in the kitchen. I uncurled my cramped limbs and launched into the internal dialogue that I depended on to propel my aching and feverish self out from under the covers each morning: *Do your yoga routine, and if you don't feel better, then you can go back to bed.* That coaxed me out of the blankets' cocoon of warmth—until my feet hit the cold floorboards. *No excuses!* I hauled my tender body upright, carefully aligned my feet under me, took a deep breath, and began the asanas to salute a new day. Soon my muscles were looser and the pain in my limbs tolerable. Once I cradled a hot cup of tea in my chilled hands, drinking in the warmth of steaming liquid, the day began to look better.

After breakfast, I headed outside. My grandmother was sitting in her overstuffed chenille armchair in the parlor perusing the newspaper; my mother was sorting through the contents of the kitchen cabinets; my dad was trimming roses and pulling weeds in the garden. I was painting.

My perch on the ladder high on the second-story wall gave a bird's-eye view of my mother's childhood home; the relatively mindless task of rolling paint across a large expanse of stucco allowed me to contemplate what this house I had grown up visiting could tell me about my mother's family and, by extension, about myself. Any data might prove useful in my quest to understand my health, so I pondered what little I knew.

Built for my grandparents just before my mom, their only child, was born in 1931, the house had always seemed to me exotic, perhaps because it was the antithesis of the bland brick suburban house in the Midwest I grew up in. From the street, my grandparents' house presented a fairly typical Mission-style bungalow face with a red tile roof and dark-stained oak front door under a tiny arched corner porch. Following the steeply sloped and very narrow driveway down the side of the house, though, its one modest story morphed into two. At the foot of the driveway was a tiny garage, and to the left, a generous archway opened in the lower-story house wall, leading to a terra-cotta-tile-floored terrace sheltered under the upper story, and from there into my grandfather's prized rose garden, and beyond that, a creek lined by fragrant eucalyptus and tall redwood trees.

A door at the corner of the covered terrace led to a spartan garden-level studio apartment once inhabited by my maternal great-grandfather Henry, whose family money likely built the house, but about whom even my mother, who grew up with his silences and his comings and goings, knows very little. Over the terrace, a window-lit second-story bridge linked the main house to a commodious two-story attached apartment that was the home of Henry's wife, my maternal great-grandmother Mira, a poet and writer of magazine and newspaper articles back when such a career was unusual for a woman.

Inside the main house were polished wood floors, French doors opening to wrought-iron balconies that overlooked the garden and the chattering creek, and niches filled with jars and baskets and vases collected on my great-grandparents' travels. My mother's piano lived in an alcove in the front parlor that was carpeted with layers of worn Persian rugs that my globe-trotting maternal great-grandfather Dr. William, a botanist, had bought on a trek through the Sahara Desert. Oils and watercolors by my maternal great-grandmother, a noted California painter who divorced Dr. William once my grandfather and his brother were grown, hung on the walls nearby. Glass-fronted cabinets in the kitchen bore stacks of hand-painted bone china plates meant to be used, no doubt, with the piles of yellowing and apparently never-unfolded damask tablecloths and matching monogrammed napkins that lay on the shelves in the cedar-paneled linen closet.

As my mother methodically emptied closets, cabinets, shelves, and niches, I took breaks from painting and helped her sort the accumulation, and pestered her with questions about my grandparents' things. She told me what she could, but most of what I saw as treasures were to her simply the furnishings of her childhood, things she had never thought to ask about.

I also volunteered to prepare meals. I like to cook, my mother can take it or leave it, and my grandmother always preferred to be waited on. My first night on duty, I fixed my grandmother's favorite meal and proudly dished up the first course—pork chops with mashed potatoes, mint jelly, and applesauce—and waited for Grandmother Janet's approval. She sent her pork chop back to be cooked until it was sufficiently chewy. After I removed the dinner plates, I served her favorite kind of Jell-O and fruit. She consumed the wobbly stuff and then remained at the table while my parents and I cleared, and after I brought out her cup of Postum coffee substitute. She sat at her place alone while I washed the dishes.

As I stacked the clean dishes in the cabinet, I heard her querulous voice from the dining room: "Where is dessert?"

After that, I always served Jell-O *and* pie.

I missed my granddad Milner. On our childhood visits, he showed my brother and me how to feed the koi in the pond in his rose garden, their soft lips nibbling our fingers. He pointed out the ripe avocados on the tree that hung over the neighbor's fence, and left the gate at the bottom of the garden open so we could slip through and explore the wilderness of the city park beyond, with its tangled woods and creek issuing from the damp cave created by the street bridge. He and my mom shared with us their favorite places from her childhood: ferry rides across the foggy bay to eat crab cocktails at Fisherman's Wharf, the enticing aromas of the Ghirardelli chocolate factory, dark stores in Chinatown where we tasted mystery delicacies pulled from ranks of shelves that rose to the ceiling, the heart-pumping stairs to Coit Tower and its view over the city, and Stinson Beach, where we skipped stones, collected shells, and chased ocean waves.

My grandfather reminds me of Aries, the magic winged ram in the Greek myth of the constellation. When their stepmother plotted to get rid of Phrixus and Helle, children of the king she had married, the gods sent Aries to the rescue, and the curly-fleeced beast flew away across the Black Sea with the children on his back. Whenever things got sticky with my grandmother, my granddad Milner whisked my brother and me off to explore some interesting place. He had done the same thing for my mother in her childhood, and the excursions they shared are some of her favorite stories of those years.

A FEW WEEKS LATER, after my grandmother's move to Tucson, my mom and I were talking on the phone. I asked how things were going.

"She's not happy," said my mom. "I can't seem to do anything right; your father, on the other hand, can do no wrong."

"Ouch," I said.

Almost every day, my grandmother would call my mom to complain: the sun was too bright for her staghorn ferns, the grocery store's pies were inedible, her neighbors parked too close to her porch. The day before, it had been her medicines: they were wrong. My mother had walked over to my grandmother's and patiently detailed what each pill was for and why she needed to take them.

"These aren't what my doctor in Berkeley prescribed," my grandmother protested. They were equivalents or newer versions, my mom explained. But my grandmother wasn't convinced. So my mom walked home and sent my dad over.

As soon as my dad appeared, my grandmother turned coquettish.

"Why didn't Joan tell me that? She just doesn't take time for me the way you do."

"I know that I should just let her slide off my back," my mom said to me. "But she makes me so mad."

Within a month, my mother began to experience serious pain in the joints of her hands. Eventually, she went to see her doctor, who referred her to a specialist. The diagnosis: degenerative rheumatoid arthritis.

Rheumatoid arthritis is a connective tissue disease classified in the same group as the illness I was diagnosed with. In fact, the two share some of the same major symptoms, including joint pain and swelling, unexplained fevers, and chronic exhaustion. In rheumatoid arthritis, however, pain progresses into deterioration, eventually resulting in limited range of motion in the affected joints—or rendering them useless altogether. Although the disease has been intensively studied, it is just as much a mystery as many other connective tissue diseases: its cause or causes are not known, the events that trigger it are not clear, there is no cure.

My mom, in her fifties then and fit and active, was not daunted. Controlling the arthritis, she figured, was simply a matter of finding the right treatment. She began with the one recommended by her rheumatologist: a weekly injection with a solution of gold salts. Gold salts are Western medicine at its most medieval. They have been used since at least the Middle Ages as a remedy for the symptoms of rheumatoid arthritis, though researchers cannot explain how or why they work beyond the fact that small doses of the precious metal sometimes suppress the immune system's production of destructive antibodies.

For almost two years, the gold salts seemed to work and my mother's arthritis remained stable, seemingly manageable—until the summer she lost 20 pounds from her 135-pound frame and, along with it, her normally indefatigable energy. After that, the arthritis progressed from joint to joint through her body: from her hands to her shoulders, to her wrists and elbows, to the balls of her feet, her knees, and her hips. With each flare-up, the affected joints swelled and grew painful, literally hot to the touch, and the skin around the joint stretched and cracked. The connective tissue that lines the joint and links muscle to bone and muscle to muscle deteriorated. Without that cushion and support, bones moved out of alignment and bone grated on bone. Some joints sprouted bone spurs; others simply disintegrated.

Before arthritis, my mom played the piano. The melodies of Bach, Handel, and Chopin thread through my childhood memories from her afternoon practices. Within a few years of the onset of the disease, her hands could no longer stretch sufficiently to span the octaves. She quit playing and eventually sold her piano. On her worst days, her hands were all thumbs and she struggled with everyday tasks like buttoning a blouse, tying a shoelace, or opening a jar. We bought her a jar opener; she switched to shoes with wide, easily grasped Velcro strips; my dad took to helping her with buttons.

ARIES CROPS UP IN Greek mythology again when Jason and his crew of Argonauts set off on a quest to recover the Golden Fleece, the winged ram's much-venerated skin, from the king who gave Phrixus shelter. (Phrixus' sister had perished when she lost her grip and drowned on their flight to safety; Phrixus' new king sacrificed the ram and kept its Golden Fleece.) After an epic journey involved man-eating Harpies, violent storms, ship-crushing straits, and a killer giant, Jason enlisted the king's daughter in stealing the Golden Fleece, and the pair and their crew made their way home to Greece, where Jason reclaimed his father's kingdom, married the girl—and then died homeless and alone, a reminder that life is not necessarily fair.

My mother's search for a drug to control her rheumatoid arthritis reads like the hero's journey Jason undertook—without the romance. After the gold salts lost their effectiveness, her joints deteriorated so rapidly that her rheumatologist, normally a conservative sort, suggested exploring other drug therapies. Helped by my dad, an organic chemist whose career centered on developing pharmaceuticals, my mom researched each treatment before trying it. As the combinations of medicines became more complicated, she began keeping a log detailing which drugs she was taking, their dosages, and notations of her symptoms.

They began with prednisone, a corticosteroid, which seemed to stem the deterioration but caused my mom to lose her appetite. She took methotrexate and other chemotherapy drugs to depress her immune system and lower the levels of connective-tissue-destroying antibodies, accompanied by massive doses of sulfasalazine and other antibiotics to kill any infections her drug-impaired immune system couldn't repel. The combination of drugs, her log notes, made her tongue so sore that she could barely talk and robbed food of taste. Her appetite dwindled. Never fat, she grew thin.

To combat the persistent pain and swelling in her joints, she took ibuprofen at the highest doses her body could tolerate, then switched to Lodine when the ibuprofen no longer worked, and eventually also tried Voltaren and other nonsteroidal anti-inflammatories. Still the pain did not diminish; she continued to lose weight and began to shrink in height as well. Her notes record her frustration at one point at being so weak that it was difficult to get out of bed each day. The pain in her joints increased so much that her doctor prescribed liquid morphine, which caused my mom to throw up uncontrollably.

She took Tagamet to counteract the corrosive effect on her stomach lining of the various painkillers and anti-inflammatories, iron for the anemia from not eating when the other drugs made her sick, calcium and salmon calcitonin to rebuild the bone mass depleted by the corticosteroids. Eventually, she had surgery to break and fuse the degraded joints in her hands, and then a few years later, her feet. Each new therapy seemed promising, and sometimes her arthritis went into remission for months or years. But it never went away. Her joints continued to deteriorate. The pain ate at her appetite and strength. Over the decades, she shrank, eventually dropping below 100 pounds and losing more than three inches in height.

NOT LONG AFTER my mom was diagnosed, I sent her a copy of *Anatomy of an Illness*, the book my doctor had assigned as homework. That began an ongoing information trade: we send each other relevant books and articles and share observations and theories. Like colleagues pursuing similar questions about which little is known, we multiply the effectiveness of our searches by exchanging information. Our communication also helps each of us feel less alone.

One thing we do not talk much about is each of our roles in the other's health. Researchers studying connective tissue diseases say that although individual illnesses are not inheritable, children of parents with connective tissue diseases may inherit the tendency to develop one of these illnesses themselves. In parent-child pairs where both have connective tissue diseases, however, the two generations usually express different illnesses. Hence my diagnosis with undifferentiated connective tissue disease, not rheumatoid arthritis like my mom, and my brother's later diagnosis with psoriasis and a form of asthma, both considered connective tissue diseases. "Inheritance" of these illnesses may also work in the opposite direction, from child to parent: the foreign cellular material of the developing fetus may trigger the potential of the illness in the mother. That my conception— or my brother's—might have predestined Mom for rheumatoid arthritis is almost too painful for me to contemplate. I suspect that the probability that my brother and I inherited her tendency to express a connective tissue disease is equally painful for my mom.

Like Rudyard Kipling's Elephant's Child, my mother and I share an insatiable curiosity. Our approaches to our respective health challenges, however, are radically different. My mom is unwavering in her resolve to try any reputable therapy offered by Western medicine and in her faith in the quest for a cure, while I instinctively listen to my symptoms instead of suppressing them, adapt to the conditions of my health rather than fight.

In a sense my approach is modeled on the organisms I studied in my fieldwork: plants. Although their lives are fundamentally unlike our own, lacking what we call eyes, lips, brains, and hearts, these rooted beings form the very fabric of life on Earth. Billions of years older than humans and our simian ancestors, plants make our lives possible: they quite literally green the Earth, shaping and softening nearly every terrestrial environment, from cracks in city sidewalks to frozen peaks in Antarctica. They are solar pioneers, using the sun's energy to synthesize the sugars life feeds on. And they are our "breathing-buddies" in the words of poet Clifford Burke, exhaling the oxygen we require and inhaling the carbon dioxide that we and our fossil-fuel-burning technologies exhale. Their collective respiration maintains the level of oxygen that is optimal for our survival; their carbon-fixing inhalations play a central role in the carbon cycle, crucial to the regulation of greenhouse gases. They are our shelter, our nurture, our sustenance.

One plant species in particular has spoken to me since I first noticed its scent in childhood: big sagebrush. This often-unloved shrub tints miles and miles of western landscapes with its gray-green foliage. Its fragrance, dominated by notes of turpentine and resin and finished with honey and orange blossoms, is so characteristic that one sniff evokes the West.

The "seas" of sagebrush covering the intermountain West originated in wrenching environmental change. Around twenty-five million years ago, the Sierra Nevada and Cascade Mountains were thrust up parallel to the Pacific coast, casting a long rain-shadow all the way to the Rocky Mountains. As the then predominant forests of maple, sweet gum, and other deciduous trees shriveled in the drought, animals—generally more mobile—moved away while less mobile plants died out, retreated uphill, or adapted, developing water-saving strategies in order to survive.

Big sagebrush "chose" to adapt, reducing the size of its three-tipped leaves, covering them with a silver-hairy insulating felt, and turning evergreen, offsetting reduced leaf area for food production by retaining those leaves year-round to capture every possible moment of sunlight. The shrub also adapted its form to suit the conditions of each site, ranging from knee-high and wind-pruned to eight feet tall and layered. And it adapted its behavior: the shrub actively reorients its foliage in response to sun and wind in order to preserve precious moisture.

Sometime in the long millennia of adaptation, big sagebrush developed a way to communicate using its signature scent. The shrub's very abundance makes it attractive to legions of grazers, from microscopic mites to half-ton ungulates. It repels these hungry hordes by making itself stink: synthesizing the complex of chemicals that produce its turpentiney fragrance, thus broadcasting an aromatic advertisement that its tissues taste bad, are difficult to digest, and can clog grazers' guts like an overdose of doughnuts. Big sagebrush eventually developed a whole vocabulary of volatile compounds, including one chemical that acts like an aromatic air-raid siren to warn its community of grazing insect invasions; when other plant species pick up this signal, they flood their tissues with indigestible compounds.

Today the shrub whose fragrance and form I so love is as critical to the health of these cold-desert landscapes as pine and fir forests are in the adjacent mountains. Like a forest overstory, the canopy provided by big sagebrush acts as a shelter: it shades the ground, protecting the surface from both searing daytimes and frigid nights, cuts the constant wind, and retards evaporation. It enriches the soil by trapping airborne dust and detritus rich in organic matter and mineral nutrients. It captures rain, channeling that precious moisture down its trunks to filter into the soil instead of sheeting off the surface, and collects its own wind-deposited mini-snowdrifts in winter to supply extra moisture in spring.

Hundreds of wildlife species depend on big sagebrush for homes and food, from pronghorn antelope and eye-catching black-and-white sagebrush sheepmoths, to the emblematic sage-grouse, which may walk tens of miles between windswept winter sagebrush range and summer habitat in moist sagebrush meadows. Without the shrub, these landscapes, often dismissed as desolate, would truly be deserted.

I'M NO BIG SAGEBRUSH. But I adopted the shrub's strategy of flexibility: restructuring my life to survive conditions I couldn't change. Take my malaise upon waking. I knew from experience that when I got out of bed and moved around, the pain that made me want to curl in a tight ball under the covers would recede; the gentle, focused exercise of yoga seemed somehow beneficial. Eventually I discovered the physiological truth that movement stimulates circulation, stirring the fluids that have pooled in place overnight to resume flowing and thus cleanse and nurture my beleaguered tissues. The nightly stagnation of circulation in sleep promotes swelling and joint pain; the accumulation of toxins may also trigger the immune system. The gentle overall stretching of my morning yoga routine restarted the flow and thus resolved the swelling and pain. I heeded my body, tuning my life to its rhythms the way big sagebrush has adapted to the shifting conditions of its harsh home.

"The impulse to *do* when sick is understandable," writes physician Larry Dossey in *Healing Words*, "and a certain amount of doing is always valuable and can even be lifesaving. But doing must also be supplemented by *being*—looking inward, examining, focusing, wondering, asking." I'm a "be-er" in response to health issues; my mom is clearly a doer. She grew up in the miracle years of medicine when sulfa drugs revolutionized the treatment of illness, seemingly wiping deadly diseases like tuberculosis from the screen of human experience. Her faith is supported by my father, a scientist with a doctorate in organic chemistry and more than a hundred patents to his name.

I have great respect for their beliefs. But I grew up in the era where antibiotics have become so overused that tuberculosis reappeared as the bacteria evolved resistance to the drugs, and where pharmaceutical-laden water from sewage plants now turns fish downstream into sterile hermaphrodites, where hospitals have become breeding grounds of flesh-eating infections, and where death by medical mistake is a serious concern. I know that medicine can perform miracles, but I don't have my mother's faith that it necessarily will.

TO MY EYES, my mom is beautiful, with large blue eyes, a cap of wavy silver hair framing her tan face, and a ready, charming smile. The notes in her health log, though, reveal the pain of swollen and distorted joints, the debilitating curve in her spine, the digits frozen or twisted into unnatural angles, her stick-thin arms and legs. She writes of the disappointment when each drug, so promising at the start, became less and less effective; of days when her body felt like a battleground.

Despite the doctrine of primum non nocere — "First do no harm" — underlying the Hippocratic oath, it seems to me that Western medicine has adopted a military mind-set, treating my mom's degenerative arthritis, for instance, by bombarding her body with a deadly variety of weapons, including chemotherapy drugs, immune-system suppressants, and antibiotics, substances that literally act against *bios*, or "life." This arsenal is directed against a disease whose cause and progression remain a mystery. The collateral damage has been my mother's health: the diminution of her bone mass and appetite, her loss of weight and physical resilience. And still her arthritis progresses undeterred; each year her joints grow more disfigured and painful, each year she loses more mobility.

Before arthritis, my mom wore three rings: her engagement diamond, a slender gold wedding band, and an antique Italian cameo passed down from her mother's aunt. When Mom's finger joints became so swollen that her rings had to be cut and bridged, she gave the cameo to me. One afternoon, I was trimming her nails. In one of the small ironies inherent in life with a chronic illness, the short and brittle nails she has always despaired of began to grow luxuriantly as a side effect of one of her medicines — just when her fused joints and twisted fingers made it impossible for her to wield a nail clipper.

As I cradled her cold and bloodless hands gingerly in mine, I was struck by the juxtaposition of our fingers, hers swollen, crooked, and painful, mine still slender and relatively straight, her cameo on my hand. I felt the stiffness in my joints and fear stabbed my gut: I saw my mother's hands in mine. And I swore that I would not allow my body to become a battleground.

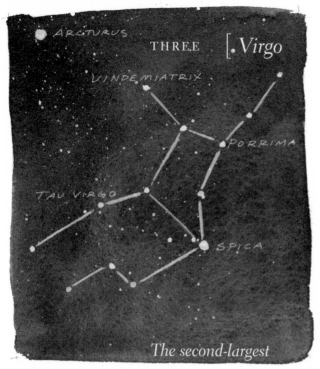

THREE

[. *Virgo*

The second-largest

constellation in the night sky represents the goddess Virgo,
named for and symbolizing virginity, that epitome of feminine
virtue. She is often pictured reclining, modestly draped in
flowing robes and bearing emblems of domesticity. In her left
hand is a sheaf of grain, marked in the sky by the constellation's
only easily recognizable star, the dazzling blue-white Spica;
her right holds a palm frond. Virgo is not completely naive,
however. The seeds and fruits of the "tame" plants she bears
arise from the distinctly untamed process of floral sex, life's
unquenchable desire to reproduce. Virgo represents the original
Earth Mother: she is responsible for the seasons, the annual
cycle of life and death. "Virgin" in the archaic sense also meant
a woman who belongs to herself, un-owned by either father or
husband, and one who has not been "deflowered."

ONE BRIGHT AND SUNNY August morning almost a year after my divorce, I stood at the Eagle Creek Trailhead, dwarfed by my bulging green backpack. Sadie, a friend's German shorthaired pointer, sat next to me, dog pack strapped on, quivering with excitement. A shutter clicked. My friend's teenage son handed my camera back to me.

"Well," he said, eyeing my overstuffed pack. "I hope you've got everything."

"If I don't," I replied, "it doesn't matter, because I can't carry another ounce."

I handed him the keys to my pickup. "The truck's yours until I get back. And there better not be a scratch on it!"

He took the keys, grinned, got in, and gunned the engine. "Be careful," he said through the open window as he backed away.

I waved as he pulled the truck onto the highway. The pickup grew smaller and smaller and then disappeared around a bend in the valley. The noise of the engine died away, and all was quiet except for the wind in the trees and the river rushing under the wooden footbridge. We were alone, with no other humans in sight. I shivered, a wave of goose bumps marching across my skin, and then shook myself. It was too late for doubts or fear.

We were forty-five miles west of Cody, just off the road to Yellowstone National Park, headed on foot from the North Fork of the Shoshone River to Jackson Hole, a distance of over a hundred miles through some of the wildest country in the lower forty-eight states. Our hike would take around seven days, depending on my walking speed and stamina. We would climb two mountain passes, including the Continental Divide, make our way through three wilderness areas, two national forests, and one national park and ford wild streams and rivers. There'd be no roads, no phones, no flush toilets, no grocery stores, no dialing 911 for emergency assistance. We'd traverse the heart of a region so untamed that it belongs more to the resident grizzly bears than to humans.

A robin-sized, gunmetal-gray American dipper warbled as it flew upstream.

"Okay, Sadie," I said to the eager dog. "Let's go."

By the time I turned, swaying a little under the weight of my heavy pack, she had dashed across the footbridge and was waiting on the other side, tail waving.

She set out up the trail in front of me. Her dog packs jiggled and her feet raised small puffs of dust as she trotted along. As she passed a boulder that stuck out into the trail, her nearside pack hit it with a thunk. She staggered and then looked back over her shoulder as if to say, "What happened?"

I chuckled, and the knots in my stomach loosened. "You're wider now, Sade." I caught up with her and patted her head. "You've got to allow more room to go around."

She scraped past the rock and headed on.

The sun was warm on my face, the air perfumed by pine sap. A red-tailed hawk circled high overhead, then screamed: ki-yeer!

"We'll be okay," I said in the quiet and followed Sadie up the trail.

I WAS BORN TO a small tribe: two parents, my brother and I, plus two pairs of grandparents, each half a continent away on opposite coasts. In my childhood home, drawers in the basement cabinets held collections of neatly labeled seashells and rock specimens. We had a black light for fluorescing minerals, a garden of native wildflowers rescued from development sites, roadkill held for study in the freezer, binoculars and a shelf of nature field guides close at hand.

Our family car was a tradesman's van converted for camping, our family lexicon rich with the names of wild plants and animals. Other kids' heads were filled with G.I. Joes, Barbie dolls, and the opening bars of "Goldfinger"; mine held the courting songs of robins, the habitat of ladies' tresses orchids, and the physics of sand dune formation. Other families' vacations took them to Disneyland or the beach; ours took us on hikes in the tangled reaches of state and national parks and wildlife refuges.

I'm the child of a research chemist turned ornithologist and a librarian interested in natural history, the sister of a fisheries biologist who is a noted bird-watcher. One grandfather was an accountant who had a passion for philosophy and a talent for horticulture; the other, a design engineer who could render the most complicated systems simple. My great-grandparents included a botanist who studied deserts the world around. Science is part of my family culture along with the connection with nature.

I am a child of Virgo as well, born in the late-summer weeks when the sun rides in the part of the sky ruled by that contradictory constellation. I am in fact doubly Virgoan, since the star grouping and I each appeared at dawn. In the language of astrology, that makes me all the more influenced by Virgo's contradictory blend of domesticity and unfettered wildness, and all the more attached to the complex Earth she stands for.

I had no intention of following the family tradition into science: I took up art, beginning in junior high with painting lessons. In high school, I fell in love with photography and the fleeting and seductive quality of light. I was headed for a degree in fine-arts photography when I met a photographer whose art was rooted in documenting science. His lab was stuffed with the latest cameras and darkroom equipment; his team took field trips to exotic places. Before I even grasped my shift in allegiance, I was working for his lab, crawling on my belly to shoot endangered wildflowers, and enrolled in courses in mycology, plant physiology, and field ecology. My notes detailed not just exposure and film speed but also habitat, range, and relationship.

It was the mid-seventies, and feminism was in the air. I hung out with activists and took part in marches. But the issues didn't seem to apply to me: I thought of myself as just one of the guys. Once, on a research outing in Big Bend National Park, my period arrived unexpectedly. I woke soaked, slithered out of my sleeping bag, and quickly wrapped myself in a jacket and slunk to the campground bathroom to clean up before my colleagues could notice.

I did everything I could to downplay my femininity. I dressed in neutral colors, favoring jeans and boots; I pinned my long hair up in a bun and hid it under a ball cap; I learned to hunt and fly-fish so that I could swap stories with my colleagues.

In my first job in field science, I was the only woman on the staff of the national forest in a "professional" position, that is, whose job involved managing natural resources, rather than managing people. The forest supervisor, a nice, fatherly sort of man, called me to his office one day. I must know, he said, that the Forest had never had a "girl" working in the field before. He wondered how I'd handle being out for days or weeks at a time with the guys. Puzzled, I replied that I didn't think it would be a problem. He pressed: Was I comfortable? Yes, I said. Had I given thought to the, ah, arrangements?

"Oh," I said, the light dawning. "No problem. They'll pee on one side of the truck; I'll pee on the other. I'll sleep in my tent; they'll sleep in theirs."

He was relieved.

Once, one of my older colleagues took me aside for some career counseling, which included suggesting—with the best of intentions, I am sure—that I limit my socializing with the "girls" (the female office staff) to avoid appearing unprofessional. After that, we took our girl-chats away from the office to living room couches and barstools.

The first time I gave a presentation on my research, I walked into the conference room at the local Game and Fish Department office, and the room was filled with guys, all in uniform—black cowboy hats, burgundy western shirts, blue jeans, and boots. I put on my most confident face.

The man at the head of the table asked without even looking up, "Honey, would you get the coffee?"

I thought for half a second and then responded sweetly, "I don't think so, honey. I'm the speaker."

He looked up, swallowed, and apologized.

I laughed. I just wanted to belong.

THE FIRST AFTERNOON on my Thorofare trek, Sadie and I had just gotten into our hiking rhythm when a sudden thunderstorm sent us scurrying for the shelter of a nearby Douglas-fir. I shrugged out of my pack and pulled on my shin-length, waterproof cagoule, tucking my legs under it for warmth. Sadie huddled close as lightning struck the slope above us, charging the air with the fertile stink of ozone.

After the storm passed, we came to the first big creek crossing. Runoff from the previous winter's above-normal snow pack had swollen the small tributary creek to a silty torrent. I eyed the water doubtfully, and then lowered myself to the gravel bank to change from my hiking boots to the old running shoes I'd brought for wading.

Sadie whined.

"It's okay, girl. It's running high, but we can make it."

Shoes on, hiking boots and socks slung around my neck, I hauled myself upright.

"Ready?" I asked Sadie. She wagged her tail.

"Okay. In we go."

The water temperature was a shock. Bone-chilling cold. The cobbles of the stream bed were slippery, the current stronger than I expected. Sadie, pacing the bank behind me, whined again.

"Come on, girl!" I commanded.

I struggled to keep my balance as I inched forward across the current. I heard her splash in, but couldn't turn to look. I was in past my knees. The bones of my feet and legs ached with the cold. Up to my thighs, and I figured I was halfway across. I couldn't see Sadie, but I figured I'd worry about her when I reached the other side. Creeping forward, my legs and feet numb, rubbery, I was nearly there.

An arm's length from the bank, I slipped into a hole invisible in the opaque water. My legs flew out from under me. My pack pulled me down. I managed to grab a spruce root protruding from the bank. For a long moment, I hung on the balance, the current tugging at me, my arms clinging tight to the rough bark. Finally I pulled myself out, soaked and shaking.

I remembered Sadie and willed numb lips to purse and tongue to whistle. To my immense relief, she appeared a ways downstream. She scrambled up the bank and galloped over, packs flapping, water streaming off her skinny body, tail wagging.

I hugged her close, and she licked my face more enthusiastically than I deserved.

"We made it!" Even my voice was shaking.

My brain clicked into survival mode. I began what would become an automatic routine after every stream we forded: Take off cumbersome pack. Peel off wet fording shoes as quickly as clumsy fingers allowed. Dry and massage numb feet and legs. Check for injuries. Put on socks and force hiking boots back on. Eat a handful of trail mix. Stand up. Move around. Examine Sadie. Haul on my pack and get back on the trail—quickly!—before the chill shut me down.

MY FIELDWORK WAS MY LIFE. It was also my niche in the sense that ecologists use the word: it was my role, my place in the community. I spent my days outdoors where the silvery and pungent oceans of sagebrush meet the Rocky Mountains, untangling the relationships that define wild plant and animal communities and deciphering the implications for human lives. I came to know intimately the wild places where elk, calypso orchids, and grizzly bears outnumber people. The more I learned, the more I felt I belonged to the place.

Except that I was always cold. In the morning, I woke curled in a tight ball, whether under the blankets at home or inside my down sleeping bag in the backcountry. Hot coffee or tea was my first conscious wish, even before food—and I'm always hungry. I lived with Thermos in hand. Still, by late afternoon, nothing could ward off the cold that slowed my body and brain.

A tendency to perpetual chill is a serious handicap for anyone, particularly anyone working far from external heat sources like furnaces, hot showers, and electric blankets. I sometimes camped out for days at a time, usually solo. I always carried a portable radio, but the rugged ridge-and-peak topography of my fieldwork area often came between the nearest antenna and me, rendering the radio mere baggage. I got so used to always being cold that on those times when the combination of chill and fatigue took over after a long day's hike, I barely noticed as I slid toward hypothermia and my movements became increasingly clumsy, my thoughts snarled in intractable knots. I survived on autopilot. I knew if I could reach my truck, I'd be okay. I always did, though I can't always remember how.

Eventually my women friends persuaded me to see a doctor. She diagnosed my chill as Raynaud's phenomenon, a circulatory ailment that causes the blood vessels of the extremities—fingers and toes, and less commonly the nose, lips, and earlobes—to constrict spasmodically, restricting or stopping blood flow. As the capillaries spasm and cells go into crisis without oxygen, the skin blanches from pink to yellow and sickly blue.

My childhood memories are tinged by blue extremities and numb lips, as are my teenage recollections of high school swim class in that chilly swimming pool. I had assumed my pallor, chattering teeth, and loss of coordination were normal until the doctor explained Raynaud's.

Raynaud's episodes can last only minutes or go on for hours; when the vessels recover, the skin flushes bright red and nerve endings sizzle. Named for French physician Maurice Raynaud, who first described the phenomenon in 1888, the symptoms can be triggered by exposure to cold, caffeine and other drugs, chronic exhaustion, and physical and emotional stress. The syndrome often accompanies connective tissue diseases.

There is nothing charming about the sickly tinge that characterizes a Raynaud's attack, although the cosmetic effects are the least serious of the syndrome's implications. With nerve connections essentially shut down by the circulatory freeze, Raynaud's sufferers can injure themselves without realizing it. Several months after I dropped the cup that led me to the doctor, I nearly sliced off the end of my index finger while cutting carrots. Alerted to the accident by the bright blood staining the carrots, I didn't feel a thing until a doctor stitched my fingertip back in place. With no anesthesia I was keenly aware of every movement of the needle through my flesh.

The chill of Raynaud's can also lead right into hypothermia, making thinking difficult and tossing logic to the winds. And years of the chronic freeze can result in nerve loss, raising the danger of frostbite, skin ulcers, gangrene, and amputation. I'm fortunate: my fingertips and toes have lost sensation over the years, but I haven't lost them.

After I dressed, the doctor and I talked. The late afternoon sun slanted in the window. I shivered, unable to get warm. She spoke in a soft voice with a marked accent of her native India; her hands danced gracefully in the air, giving shape to her words. I took notes until she began giving advice: I should find indoor work or, better still, move to a warmer climate.

I put down my mechanical pencil to protest. I loved my field-work, loved being outside. I couldn't imagine leaving the mountains and sagebrush country.

She frowned. "There are things you cannot see. The paleness of your skin—you have the yellow of jaundice almost, and always so cold. You must watch yourself, treat yourself carefully, for when you are tired, you have the tinge of dying in the yellowness."

She might have been speaking in tongues for all I could comprehend.

"You look like the dying," she continued. "Tired enough, your body could believe in its own illness. We all carry our death with us—yours perhaps more close, more powerful than others."

Of course I'm dying, I thought. I have a connective tissue disease. What's her point? I wanted data, not metaphysics. I thanked her politely and went back to work.

WHEN I LOOK UP AT the myriad stars in summer night skies, I search for the brilliant shine of Spica to locate the dim and sprawling form of Virgo, the constellation I was born to. With a luminosity two thousand times that of our own sun, Spica is the brightest star in the Northern Hemisphere summer sky. It is also hot, burning at temperatures around 36,000 degrees Fahrenheit. If it were nearby, this huge star—ten times more massive than our sun—would outshine every celestial body in the night sky; we would be able to read by its light even on moonless nights. We would also incinerate. Fortunately for life on Earth, Spica lies 270 light-years away, sufficient to assuage the star's fire. (A light-year is the distance light travels through space in a year. The light we see from Spica left that star 270 years ago.)

I may have been physically cold, but my emotions burned with Spica's white-hot glow. I clung to my professional niche, but I couldn't seem to hold my personal life together. I was dying; why care? I fell in with a hard-drinking barrel racer, traveling with her on the weekend rodeo circuit until the night she jackknifed her horse trailer into a roadside ditch and laughed herself sick after we crawled out of the wrecked pickup; I kayaked fierce rapids and skied crazy runs; I slept with men I barely knew. The fire that drove me erased my caution and also my memory—whole sections of years are lost beyond recall.

One thing stands out clearly: the weekly column on nature I had begun writing and illustrating for the local newspaper. It was only a summer assignment, and it barely paid. But as I struggled to capture the forms of the plants I knew intimately in precise pen lines and wrestled just the right words to illuminate the relationships that make up what Aldo Leopold called "the community of the land," a door opened. This work felt right when everything else did not. If I couldn't practice science and stay healthy, perhaps I could write about it. But first I would have to learn how. One weekend, I paid a visit to an environmental newspaper in another town and talked them into taking me on as an unpaid intern. When I returned home, I resigned from my job, gave my landlord notice, and told my friends I was leaving.

The January day of my move dawned with blizzard warnings. On my way out of town, I stopped to say good-bye to a close friend. He walked me to my car, then pulled me into his arms and leaned back on the fender.

"Stay. I have room. I'd take care of you."

"I can't."

"Won't," he said, blue eyes pinning mine. "You're running away."

I pulled out of his embrace and got into the car.

A layer of low clouds shrouded the sky as I drove south, leaking a steady rain of snowflakes that streamed across the highway like shreds of icy fog. My compact wagon bucked in the wind; my hands shook as I gripped the steering wheel.

At the newspaper, I discovered that the pace of journalism was too quick for me. I needed more time to find the story—and my voice—than newspaper deadlines allowed. I was bunking with one of my editors; she made it clear that she needed my rent payments but not my friendship. I found part-time work cleaning houses and began lingering in the empty rooms after I finished, sitting in the dark and inhaling their fragrances, warming myself in the ashes of other's lives.

One weekend in spring, I drove to the mountains for some cross-country skiing. On the way back, I lost control of my car, skidded, and careened into a snowbank. The car was totaled, the friend riding with me sustained a neck injury, and I came away with a cracked collarbone and a dislocated shoulder. I rode the icy commute to the newspaper by bicycle until I found a room to rent in town and my parents lent me the money for a used pickup.

The following summer, I got a part-time job as director of the Women's Center at the University of Wyoming in Laramie. I found a room in a graduate-student household on the edge of the park where I had once stopped to watch the stars, just a few blocks from the place where Kent and I had been living when our lives began to part. I registered for graduate classes in science and writing, organized my new office, and started planning fall semester programs. I was, I thought, managing well. Until I slept. Night after night, I failed to catch the blue cup, I saw the wall vibrate as Kent slammed the door, I sat in the doctor's office waiting for her to speak, I plunged my hands into the sink full of icy water, I watched Kent's jaw harden, I saw my mother's hands in mine. Finally, I borrowed Sadie and ran away.

The night before our trek, I stayed with a friend from the Forest Service. After dinner, we sat in her comfortable living room, drinking wine and trading stories.

"What brings you home at this time of year?" She swirled the wine in her glass.

I told her about my planned trip: "I'm taking a break to think about things."

Her usual cheerful smile disappeared and she shook her head with a bouncy motion, like a disturbed chickadee. "Who's going with you?"

I looked away. "Well—" I couldn't think of a lie. "Everybody is busy or out of town, and I really need to go. So I'm taking Sadie for company."

Her anger hit me like a slap in the face. "A week on foot and alone in that country with your health—that's just stupid! No, not just stupid. It's dangerous!"

She paused, as if expecting me to defend myself.

"You won't listen to me, or anyone else. You'll go anyway."

I looked away. She was right on both counts. A solo trek is dangerous, and I would go anyway. I had already reviewed the grim possibilities: I could fall, break a leg, and be unable to walk; I could be attacked by a moose or a grizzly bear, drown fording a creek, be struck by lightning on a ridge. The stress of the trip could trigger a flare-up of my illness, stranding me with only Sadie for help, miles from anywhere in a maze of roadless mountains. I'd have no way to contact anyone, much less how to find me. If I died, no one would likely find my body before the legions of flesh-eaters devoured it.

Each time I thought about it, knots formed in my stomach and I forced my mind away. There was no point in scaring myself. I was determined to go, and I had to go alone.

I slept lightly that night and woke in time to watch the stars disappear in the spreading dawn. Over breakfast, my friend agreed to let her teenage son drive me to the trailhead. Then she hugged me and left for work without another word.

WHEN I AM STUCK and cannot dig myself out of my problems, I go home to nature. I head for wild country, for someplace where I can hear myself think. I'm following a venerable tradition of seekers, including an Englishman whom some thought crazy and whose quest still speaks to me.

In the 1640s, a nineteen-year-old English apprentice named George Fox set off in search of his spiritual voice during a time of great intellectual ferment. The invention of the printing press had made the written word in the Bible widely accessible for the first time, and literacy, formerly restricted to priests and the wealthy, was spreading to common folk like Fox. The result was an explosion of new religious sects: Lutherans, Anabaptists, Puritans, Mennonites, Seekers, Rangers, Shakers, Levelers. Instead of heading for desert or mountaintop, Fox aimed for this unexplored spiritual territory.

After four years of traveling among the various sects — listening, fasting, and reading his Bible — Fox was exhausted and disillusioned. Finally, standing alone on a rocky summit in northern England, he heard a voice that spoke directly to his heart, a voice that he believed to be "that of God within us." In that transcendent moment, Fox realized that the wisdom he sought came not from preachers, priests, or ministers but from within himself, from a personal connection to the divine that was accessible to everyone. The young Englishman set off to walk throughout his land, spreading the word that all people, rich or poor, educated or not, clergy or laborer, could know the world of God if only they would be still and listen. Fox's revelation spawned the Religious Society of Friends, better known as Quakers, from early Friends' tendency to quiver with strong emotion during worship.

I began attending Quaker Meeting in high school during the Vietnam War, attracted by Friends' peace testimonies. I stayed for the simplicity of the spiritual ritual: traditional Friends' services draw on silence, with no liturgy or formal program proscribing the times for prayer, singing, or sermons, and no paid preachers. Friends gather on simple benches or chairs in plain meetinghouses and listen together for the "small, still voice" of God. The immediacy of that spiritual relationship and the richness of the collective attentiveness to listening from the silence have held me ever since.

I was once terrified of silence; I've come to thirst for it, or at least for the peace that comes when the busyness of life stills. "True silence," wrote Quaker William Penn, ". . . is to the spirit what sleep is to the body, nourishment and refreshment." Stillness and quiet are undervalued resources, rarities in landscapes dominated by humans and our attendant noise.

Nature itself is not actually silent: the wild world is as full of sound as it is of life. But its sounds — the whooshing of wind in evergreen boughs, the haunting calls of sandhill cranes, the rasp of a grasshopper's jaws, the scream of a hunting hawk — sing the rhythms and cadences of life living itself. They beat with the same rhythms of our bodies, unlike the constant, adrenaline-pumping din generated by our beeping and thumping and roaring technology. Incessant noise overwhelms the quiet voice of our inner wisdom. That barrage was one reason I could not hear myself think.

ONE LUNCHTIME MIDWAY through our trek, Sadie and I sprawled on the grassy banks of the Thorofare River, dogged by clouds of whining mosquitoes. I munched my crackers and cheese, trying not to inhale protein in the form of flying insects, and scanned the lush expanse of meadow across the water, where a long-necked and long-legged sandhill crane nearly as tall as I probed the soil for food. A large dark form crept along behind the bird, belly low to the ground, the way a dog stalks a magpie. When the stalker came within range, it launched itself into the air, leaping for the crane. The crane lifted off on wide wings and flew away, trumpeting its resonant call. The stalker thudded to earth. The crane circled, then landed nearer to Sadie and me and resumed feeding. The furry one resumed its creeping approach. I sat riveted by the drama, until my brain belatedly registered the stalker as a grizzly bear.

I rose quietly, lunch in hand, heaved on my pack, and motioned Sadie to follow. I tiptoed backward, silent, eyes on the bear. It was all I could do to keep myself from breaking into a run. The bear raised its shaggy head and looked across the river. Sadie and I froze. Sweat trickled between my shoulder blades. Finally, the bear looked away.

We reached the trail and walked oh-so-casually into the screen of a grove of spruces before I drew a breath. I was shaking. I forced myself to hike on, cursing myself steadily under my breath. What had I been thinking? I might consider grizzly bears as relatives, but a grizzly had no such warm feelings: Sadie and I were interlopers at best; at worst, simply prey.

THAT EVENING WE CAME TO the largest ford of our trek, a tributary of the Thorofare River. I followed the trail to the crossing marked on the map, arriving just as the sun's slanting light gilded the landscape, laying shadows of the lodgepole pines like logs across the path. I walked up to the bank—and there the trail ended. At the foot of a raw, newly eroded bluff a silty river roared by instead of the creek I expected. For a long moment I stood there, staring at the torrent of water. Then I put down my pack, whistled for Sadie, and hiked upstream, searching for a likely crossing. No luck. Tired now, I hiked back downstream again, passing the trail and my pack, but found no likely spot to ford.

Blue with Raynaud's, I pulled myself together. I pitched my tiny tent, lit the stove, fed Sadie, and boiled water for my dinner. As I ate my ramen noodles, I pulled out the map. Upstream it showed impassible cliffs, downstream the deep Thorofare River; in front, the creek too high to attempt on foot. We were boxed in. The only way out was to go back, retracing our journey of the past several days and returning to the trailhead where we began.

I studied the map searching for a solution until darkness erased its fine, undulating lines. Then I crawled into my sleeping bag, near tears. Sadie curled up next to me. The water roared in my ears. Large animals—I hoped they were only moose—crashed through the forest nearby. My mind circled and fretted. Sometime in the night, I unzipped the tent door and poked my head out to scan the sky for stars. I peered intently seeking a glimpse, however faint, of the constellations. The night was overcast, the heavens unreadable.

WHEN I EXAMINE THE STARS, I'm not just looking for the myths and dreams we assign to the scattershot figures of the constellations, or for the flares of exploding supernovas, the sheen of gassy nebulae and milky veils of interstellar dust, or other hints of the formation of the universe. I'm seeking a kind of intuitive wisdom that my rational mind struggles to accept, much less explain. I recognize it in astrology, the study of coincidences between human lives and the movements of the stars and planets. Unexplainable and sometimes unfathomable, this system of knowledge is frequently so oversimplified that it becomes trivial, meaningless. Yet at its richest, it can ring eerily true, regardless of whether we can currently grasp what could possibly link planet and personality.

Astrology first cropped up in the cultures that inhabited the fertile crescent bounded by the Tigris and Euphrates rivers around 1400 to 1000 BC, in what is now war-blasted Iraq. Evidence of this careful observation and interpretation of astronomical phenomena appears around the world, from Persia, Egypt, and Greece, through Africa, to North and South America, Asia, India, Australia, and the Pacific Islands. In European cultures, astrology and astronomy were one discipline until the Age of Enlightenment separated them, embracing the study of the observable movements and features of the heavens while condemning the concurrences of astrology to the realm of myth and magic.

Some of science's greatest leaps have come through just the sort of intuitive connections that underlie astrology: Newton and his perhaps apocryphal falling apple illuminating the laws of gravity, for example, or Watson and Crick "seeing" the double-helix form of DNA before it was revealed by empirical models. Just because we can't see why something works doesn't mean it doesn't. What if we redefined science as "a body of knowledge used to understand the world"? We'd allow other types of wisdom—including the intuitive voices of body and soul—a respected place in our system of knowledge. I see the world through a scientist's eyes; I also read my horoscope in the daily newspaper. And when I am outside at night I look to the heavens to read the stars, searching for continuity in their timelessness, and for wisdom in their movements and the chronicles they carry.

THE NEXT MORNING, I rose early in a golden dawn, the forest around me sparkling with crystalline frost. Too miserable to admire these gifts, I ate a quick breakfast while pacing the bank above the creek. I looked at the map again and then admitted defeat. Sadie and I started off down the trail, headed back to where we'd begun at Eagle Creek.

About half a mile along, we met a backcountry angler, the first human we'd seen in days. I stopped to chat, my voice rusty with disuse. He asked where we were going, and I poured out my frustration.

"Yeah, that crossing washed out this spring," he said. "Last winter we had so much snow that all the creeks are still running high. Bad luck for you."

He thought for a moment. "There's a place down the creek where you might be able to cross, just above the confluence with the river. The flow's really wide there, but it's shallower than at the trail crossing. I've done it on horseback."

A glimmer of hope lightened my mood. I pulled out my map, and he pointed to the spot. "Good luck!" he called as we walked away.

My spirits rose as Sadie and I set out cross-country. Soon we were threading through head-high willow thickets. I sang loudly to warn bears of our approach.

We emerged on a broad gravel bar, and there was the creek, rushing past in a channel perhaps fifteen yards across, far wider than any stream we'd managed yet. I paced up and down beside the flow, scanning the current and attempting to read the creek bottom. I calculated the distance above the river and how likely we were to get washed into its deep waters.

Sadie sat, waiting.

Finally, I decided. We could do it.

I plopped down on the gravel, took off my boots and socks, and cinched my fording shoes. Then I looped a piece of nylon cord around the straps on Sadie's dog packs and tied the end to my waist so she wouldn't be swept away.

In we waded. The icy water had already reached my thighs when Sadie, paddling frantically, hit the end of her cord. I willed my legs to hold her weight, and kept going, leaning upstream. The water crept toward my crotch. I hitched up my backpack and kept going. My legs and feet were numb, but I forced myself to stumble along. Finally, soaking wet and shivering, I staggered out on the opposite side. I grabbed Sadie and twirled her in a dizzy circle before my legs collapsed under me.

TWO NOONTIMES LATER, we sat in the shade of a spreading Douglas-fir tree above the Buffalo Fork of the Snake. The path behind led into the wilderness we'd hiked through; just ahead lay the end of the trail.

"We made it!" I said to Sadie.

I opened my dusty pack and celebrated by sharing the last of my food: four RyKrisp crackers, which I carefully smeared with the last dabs of peanut butter, topped with the remaining crumbles of cheese, and dotted with a scattering of hard raisins. I set two crackers in front of Sadie. She gulped them immediately and then delicately licked her jowls.

I ate one slowly and left the other balanced on my knee, savoring this final backcountry meal. The air smelled like sun-warmed evergreen sap and dust kicked up by our feet. A breeze whooshed through the branches overhead; the river tumbled by far below. A white-breasted nuthatch called, "Yank! Yank! Yank!" then fell silent.

TO THE GREEKS, Virgo was the goddess Demeter, whose desperate search for her daughter Persephone plunged Earth into winter. When Demeter found her daughter and rescued her from the underworld, spring and life returned to the planet, but only temporarily; each autumn, Persephone honors her bargain with Hades and returns to the darkness, bringing another winter.

Like Demeter, I was searching for something so precious that its loss pushed me into the wilderness: my life—without the sentence of undifferentiated connective tissue disease. I had set out alone in the hope that I would hear a voice speaking from the silence, a revelation that would somehow guide me. Instead, what filled my head through the solitary days and nights were loneliness, fear, and anger. *Surely those were not the voices I had trekked into the wild to hear.*

SADIE WHINED. The breeze pushed a small cumulus cloud over the sun, its shadow sweeping like a giant hand across the ridge where we sat. The shadow passed, and the sun's warmth returned.

The sense that we call "hearing" involves both mechanics, the workings of the hairs and nerve endings that receive sounds and transmit them to the brain, and discernment, the mental processing necessary to focus on and interpret a particular sound from the welter of signals that bombard us. I think of listening as more the latter, the attentive part of hearing. It is the kind of intense, sustained focus that geneticist Barbara McClintock employed to parse the workings of genes in corn plants. Her research redefined the study of genetics and eventually won the scientist who had worked solo for decades following her intuitive leadings in the face of derision from colleagues a Nobel Prize. "I don't really feel like I know the story if I don't watch the plant all the way along. So I know every plant in the field," McClintock says in Evelyn Fox Keller's biography, *A Feeling for the Organism*. "I know them intimately, and I find it a great pleasure to know them."

Apparently I didn't know myself intimately, if I was surprised by the feelings I heard in the silence of my journey. It seemed I hadn't been observing myself with acuity. Perhaps that was the message in the chill of Raynaud's: slow down, thaw out, sit still, and listen. When the doctor said that we carry our death within us, mine "more close, more powerful than others," she spoke from intuitive wisdom; tuned to logic, I couldn't understand her words. Clearly I had been hearing only some of the signals, interpreting only part of the message.

Walking the days alone but for Sadie had forced me to pay attention. If I kept my awareness tuned within, I might yet hear what I needed to understand my health and, more importantly, my life.

SADIE WHINED AGAIN. Then, with an audible "gulp!" she reached forward and ate my remaining cracker.

So much for contemplation.

I laughed and ruffled her ears. "You're right. It's time to go."

I picked up my pack, lighter now than it had been when we set out on the trek, and settled it on my bruised shoulders one last time. I stood up and turned to look back up the trail we'd come on.

"Thanks for the gift of the quiet," I said to the landscape.

Then I turned and headed downhill. Sadie pranced in front of me, her feet raising small puffs of dust as we walked out of the wilderness.

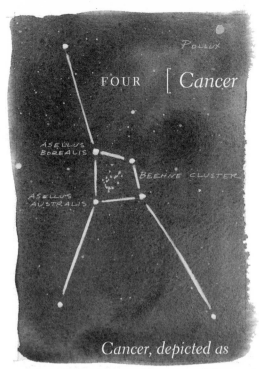

FOUR

[*Cancer*

POLLUX

ASELLUS
BOREALIS

BEEHIVE CLUSTER

ASELLUS
AUSTRALIS

Cancer, depicted as

a crab with pincers reaching toward the southern horizon, is
one of the smallest star groupings in the northern sky. Even
when it is directly overhead at night in summer, its stars are
too distant to be easily visible without magnification. Cancer's
importance lies in its connection to natural cycles. This
insignificant constellation once marked a critical point in
the year: when Cancer and the sun rose together, their transit
announced the summer solstice, the longest day of the year,
after which Earth turned toward winter. To the Egyptians the
constellation represented a scarab beetle, a jewel-colored insect
that harvests balls of fresh animal dung to feed to its larvae. Just
as the constellation once marked a turning point in the year, the
beetles occupy a critical turning point in the flow of matter and
energy by transforming animal waste into new life.

I DON'T REMEMBER my first hike, a four-mile ramble along the bluffs of the Mississippi River. But I remember the ride home: I can still see my parents scooted together on the front seat of the family car, a Ford coupe, while my brother, almost four, and I, not quite two, are stretched out head-to-head on the back seat, ready to nap. I smell the woolen musk of the car upholstery under my cheek, hear the quiet murmur of my parents' voices, and see the backs of their heads, tilted close.

Togetherness and travel dominated the pattern in the fabric of my childhood. Our trips began when Mom arrived home from work on Friday afternoons. She would fix a picnic dinner, and we would stow our gear—food, sleeping bags, knapsacks, field guides, clothing—in our camper van, a tradesman's van into which my dad had fitted a cozy traveling home with help from my granddad Olav. When my dad returned from work, we'd pile into the camper and set off.

As chief navigator, Mom sat up front next to Dad, reading maps with her magnifying glass as he drove. My brother and I sat in the dinette, playing cards, reading, bickering when we got bored. My dad, eager to make tracks toward our eventual destination, would drive late into the night. Bill and I would resist sleep as long as possible, watching the dark landscape and the sporadic lights of towns and farmhouses until we finally succumbed to the soporific rhythm of the tires on the road. Dad would drive until Mom could no longer keep him awake, and then park the van in some unobtrusive spot.

We'd wake in the morning in the warm cocoons of our sleeping bags, not remembering going to bed at all, and peer out the van windows to see where we'd ended up. It might be the edge of a farm road, an abandoned gravel quarry, a cemetery, or even a campground. Sometimes the unfamiliar landscape was spectacular: the Rocky Mountains thrusting out of the Great Plains, the cliffs above the Pacific Ocean. Other times, like the night the park rangers at Cape Cod woke us in the wee hours because we were parked at a picnic area where camping wasn't allowed, the morning's view was the used-car lot in a nearby town where Dad had hidden the camper. Always, the interior view was the same: my mom and dad curled up together, close even in sleep.

AFTER SADIE AND I WALKED out of the Thorofare, she returned to her life as a field geologist's companion and I to my graduate classes, Women's Center programs, a household that included both a flock of urban chickens and enough rock jocks to pioneer climbing routes up the interior walls of our house when the weather was too miserable to scale real cliffs.

Still, I was lonely.

I ached for a pair bond like that of my parents. But every potential relationship fizzled after I felt obligated to disclose my grim diagnosis and prognosis. It's not a subject that lends itself to intimacy: "I've been diagnosed with a terminal illness. I might live two years, or perhaps five or ten. Want a beer?" Whether the guy-of-the-moment expressed sympathy or horror or was simply speechless, discomfort edged out connection.

That Christmas, I headed to Tucson to visit my parents. One night, I called my house in Laramie. My best friend, Dale, keeper of Sadie, answered the phone.

"Who is this Rich-uhd guy?" she asked immediately, pronouncing the name with an exaggerated Georgia drawl. "He sent you a postcard. We put it on the refrigerator."

"You put it on the refrigerator! It's my mail."

"Not in this household, honey chile." She laughed.

"What does it say?" I asked, curiosity barely overcoming embarrassment.

"Ah enjoyed meetin' you at Sue's buthday din-uh," she drawled. "Ah look forwuhd to gettin' togethuh when Ah get back to Lar-uh-mie."

Richard was my friend Sue's project. Whenever Sue, a graduate student in economics, came across the street to volunteer at the Women's Center, she touted Richard's virtues like a used-car salesman working a deal. Over glasses of wine as we collated freshly copied newsletters, Sue bragged about his brilliance in classes; as we licked stamps, she plugged his generosity in helping the other econ grad students; as we sorted for bulk-mail distribution, she went on about his pride in his toddler daughter; as we walked boxes of newsletters to the campus post office, she cited his enjoyment of hiking and the out-of-doors.

"He's perfect for you."

"I'm not in the market."

Undaunted, Sue contrived an "accidental" meeting one afternoon in the beer garden of the Student Union. I am told that I was friendly, but I must have been powerfully unaware; I have no memory of the encounter at all.

In mid-December, Sue threw herself a birthday dinner at a local restaurant. When I walked in, the only seat remaining was—of course—next to Richard.

I didn't fall in love at first sight. It took me at least half an hour. It wasn't his looks, which were nothing to sneeze at: he stood six feet tall, with a well-muscled body, silky black hair, olive skin, high cheekbones, and hazel eyes under long lids. It wasn't his brain, which, one of his professors told me later, had made him the most promising student in his program. It was his heart: when Richard smiled, I felt the warmth of it in my bones. And he listened when I talked.

The postcard message was both a relief and a disappointment. Was he interested or not? I couldn't tell. Should I respond? I was afraid to guess.

After the holidays, he called. I invited him to dinner. If my household liked him, I figured I'd see what happened. He graciously ate Crock-Pot stew I had prepared from a very tough rooster that met an untimely end upon crowing too early the previous morning, and he laughed at the story. That qualified for a unanimous thumbs-up. We arranged a date, a trip to the hot springs at Saratoga, across the Snowy Range.

As I negotiated the icy curves of the highway in my blue Datsun pickup, we sat elbow-to-elbow in the cramped cab and talked nonstop. It was like catching up with an old friend I hadn't seen in a long time. As we passed Sheep Mountain, Richard talked about hiking the length of its high ridge; I talked about the long-ago fires that had sprouted the dog-hair-dense stands of pines in the forest we passed through; we compared notes on the unusual dance floor on springs in the bar of a nearby town. When the shimmering white peaks of a distant mountain range rose into view, we talked about beauty, how to value it in the monetary sense, and about how a landscape can just grab you by the heart and not let go.

We continued the conversation in the hot springs as we floated under a gray sky shedding snowflakes that sizzled when they hit the steaming water. Later, relaxed and wrinkled, we headed to the Wolf Hotel for dinner. By the time we had devoured our food, we had covered my divorce and his daughter, Molly. When we stepped out into the black winter night after dinner, we stopped in the middle of the dark street, hand in hand, to gawk at the dazzling sky full of stars, so close and so bright. On the road home, I let him take the wheel of the truck I never let anyone else drive and surprised myself by falling asleep with my head on his shoulder.

After that date, we were an item. We held hands wherever we walked. We talked about the future in terms of "we" instead of "I." Friends teased us at the suddenness of our pairing; some of my colleagues at the Women's Center lectured me on my haste. Richard didn't care. He trusted what he felt, he said. I wasn't as certain. What I felt most clearly was my heart, thumping in a cadence as wild and joyous as the blissful feet of Snoopy, Charlie Brown's beagle, flying in a doggie dance. On the plus side, there was the look in Richard's eyes when I entered the room, the feel of his hand automatically reaching for mine, the heat of our lips, the way our bodies fit together like two halves of a whole. And the sense that we'd known each other our whole lives rather than only a few weeks. Still, I needed something quantifiable, some data to support the conclusion my feelings seemed to indicate: this was love.

FALLING IN LOVE at first sight may in fact be a biological reality, an instant recognition impelled by our genes and expressed in the subtle language of the aromatic compounds that define our chemical individuality. Research shows that women choose mates in part by smell, not the fragrance of aftershave, cologne, or shampoo, but the essential odor of a man's body. That odor gives clues to the makeup of his immune system, especially one critical set of genes called the major histocompatibility complex. This gene region contains the instructions for manufacturing a diverse range of protein molecules called human leukocyte antigen proteins, whose function is to grab antigens—suspicious particles or molecules, including bacteria and viruses—floating inside the cell and carry them outside for inspection and disposal by passing immune system molecules. Different human leukocyte antigen protein molecules lock into different antigens. Thus, the more diverse the genes in a person's major histocompatibility complex, the more kinds of human leukocyte antigen protein "tools" in their molecular toolkit, and the greater their chances of disposing of harmful antigens and remaining healthy. In order to give her offspring the best shot at survival and thus of passing on her genes, a woman needs a mate whose histocompatibility complex contains instructions for tools her own lacks.

How does a woman pry into the genetic contents of her potential mate's major histocompatibility complex? Smell. The proteins synthesized by the genes in this complex affect our body odor. Research shows that women invariably prefer the scent of men whose immune complexes are complementary to their own. We sniff our way to love. And when we find the right smell, our bodies know it in a way that words cannot express. How much of the delight that Richard and I knew together as new lovers was that wordless communication passed between us as we lay together, pressed skin-to-skin, breathing in the sweaty scents of each other's bodies?

Odors play a crucial role in the mating rituals of many species. Flowering plants, unable to move about to select their partners, are the masters of scent courtship, releasing aromatic chemicals on the air to signal their desirability to the animals that act as intermediaries by transporting their pollen. Insects employ pheromones, pungent sexual attractants, to broadcast their mating pleas on the winds. Dogs, both wild and domestic, read the health and fitness of potential partners by sniffing oral and anal exhalations. Fish pour their flavors into the water; snakes taste the air with flickering tongues; mammals of many species rub musky messages on rocks, trees, and other scent posts. We humans spend millions of dollars each year on perfumes, aftershave lotions, fancy soaps, essential oils, and scented candles, even though our ability to perceive odors is pitifully limited. Our noses possess around 5 million smell-sensing cells; dogs, for comparison, canvas the air with something like 125 to 300 million.

Richard and I fit as if our bodies recognized each other at the molecular level. If the subtle scents of his immune complex complemented mine, however, promising those human leukocyte antigen proteins I lacked, I couldn't assimilate that sensory data. My intuition cried, "Go ahead!" while my intellect countered, "Hold back."

I did hold back: I didn't tell Richard about my illness. That lie by omission weighed increasingly heavily on me until one windy March afternoon when I asked him if he had time for a talk.

We walked downtown hand in hand, leaning into the waves of air that poured through the streets. We stopped at a gourmet candy store and splurged on two chocolate truffles, smooth and fat and decadent. Then we headed for the steamy warmth of a café, found a table by the window, and ordered coffee. As we fed each other bites of chocolate so rich that it exploded on my tongue, I told him the story of my diagnosis, symptoms, research, and prognosis.

"It's not clear how long I'll live. It might be two years, might be ten." My voice trailed off, and I looked down at my napkin, pleated between nervous fingers.

His hands slipped over my cold ones, his long fingers warm and strong.

"Suz," he said, his voice rough.

I looked up. Tears leaked out of the corners of his eyes, sliding down his cheeks in wet ribbons to disappear into his beard. My own eyes watered.

"It doesn't matter how long you live. I don't care if you're sick or what's ahead. I love you. Nothing can change that."

I gripped his hands tightly.

"Thank you," I whispered, and suddenly I knew: "I love you, too."

RICHARD WAS BORN when the sun was traveling in Cancer, that distant and difficult-to-discern constellation. Today Cancer is primarily known not for its historic connection with the summer solstice, but for the stellar treasure hidden in the misty smudge just visible with the naked eye between the constellation's two central stars: the Beehive Cluster, one of the earliest-recognized astronomical features. What looks simply like shimmer of stellar mist at first glance shows as a sparkling group of dozens of distinct stars through binoculars, like a swarm of stellar bees; hence the name.

The cluster is more formally known as M44, the *M* honoring Charles Messier, an eighteenth-century French comet-hunter who, while searching the heavens for orbiting balls of cosmic debris, compiled a list of hundreds of "noncomets," stellar objects that might be mistaken for comets. The Beehive Cluster is the forty-fourth such object he cataloged. (Since it was known long before then, Messier may have included it simply to lengthen his list over that of a rival astronomer.) Peering at the star cluster hidden in the unassuming constellation through a high-powered telescope reveals several hundred stars in a variety of colors and intensities, a find as startling and joyous as suddenly finding love when you weren't expecting it.

ONE MORNING A FEW MONTHS LATER, I woke feeling feverish and achy. I hauled myself out of bed, dismissing the symptoms as simply the usual. By noon, though, I was back in bed, my muscles racked with pain and my body temperature spiking at 103 degrees. My limbs began to tingle, as if they were falling asleep. I called Richard. I could feel the blood draining from my hands and feet. As he began to massage my limbs, my muscles spasmed. My arms froze, and then my legs. I couldn't move.

Richard yelled down the stairs to one of my housemates: "Call the ambulance! Susan's having some kind of seizure!"

Soon I heard sirens. Paramedics rushed upstairs. While they took my blood pressure and other readings, Richard quickly told them what had happened. I concentrated on breathing: pull the air in, push it out, in, out. The paramedics loaded me on a chair and carried me carefully down the narrow stairs and into the ambulance for the trip to the hospital.

By the time the doctor parted the curtains around my bed in the emergency room later, I was shivering. He covered me with a blanket and then sat down beside me, holding one of my numb hands in his.

"Tell me about your medical history," he said, rubbing my hand gently.

He listened to my halting recitation, interrupting occasionally with questions. By the time I finished, the seizure had passed.

"It looks like you got dehydrated from the fever," he said, "began hyperventilating, and then, because your tissues had lost so much water, your muscles seized up."

He looked down at my chart and then back at me.

"The blood tests we ran show a borderline result for the antinuclear antibody test. But that doesn't necessarily mean you don't have a connective tissue disease. You could be in remission."

At my puzzled look, he explained: "We've learned these diseases may go into remission for long periods."

It wasn't clear why this happened, he continued. But he thought it could be the case with me. "It doesn't mean that the illness is gone, but its effects may be less noticeable."

Then he asked, "Can I get anything for you?"

"Richard." My voice was hoarse. "He's out in the waiting room. I want him to hear this."

In a few minutes, the doctor returned with Richard, who gathered me into his arms while the doctor repeated what he'd told me.

"I'm going to release you," he finished, "but I want you to call in the morning before my shift is over to check in with me."

As Richard lowered me into a waiting wheelchair, tucking a blanket around me, the doctor smiled. "There's a lot we don't know about these diseases. It's possible that yours could go away permanently, if you learn to take good care of yourself."

"Thank you," I said, blinking back tears.

Halfway home, I turned to Richard: "Did you hear him? Maybe I'm not dying after all."

He pulled the car over to the side of the street and put his arms around me.

"Maybe love can cure you," he said, and kissed me.

Then he handed me his handkerchief and drove us home.

LOVE CAN HEAL. Scientists studying heart and blood vessel disease at Ohio State University, for instance, bred a group of rabbits to develop both hardening of the arteries and coronary artery disease. The bunnies were then fed a killer high-fat diet, but when they were dissected at the end of the study, researchers were puzzled to discover that a significant group of them showed no trace of coronary artery disease. Finally, the grad student who fed the lab rabbits confessed that at mealtimes, she took these rabbits out of their cages to pet and play with them. Subsequent studies replicated this result: the animals that received loving attention came out clean.

In *Molecules of Emotion*, neurobiologist Candace Pert describes how this could occur. The chemicals that produce our feelings are circulated to individual cells throughout our bodies. These molecular messages "come cruising along" through the fluids surrounding each cell, while receptors on the cell membrane "dance and vibrate" in invitation. Once a molecule of emotion binds to a cell-surface receptor, the receptor transmits its chemical message into the cell's interior, initiating activities that can have a profound affect not only on the cell, says Pert, but also on the organism as a whole, translating to changes in behavior, physical activity, mood, and overall health. Love can truly change us from within.

A MONTH AFTER THAT rushed trip to the hospital, Richard and I married in a simple ceremony in the manner of Quakers, with my parents, our closest friends, and four-year-old Molly in attendance. Before that ceremony could occur, Richard had to get a divorce from Molly's mother. That process dragged on so long that the actual decree wasn't signed until the Thursday before our planned Saturday wedding. That Friday afternoon we found ourselves sitting on the "lovers' bench" in the Albany County courthouse with Molly, applying for our marriage license.

The clerk asked each of us a series of questions ending with: "Were you married before?"

When I answered yes, she asked where and when was I divorced.

"Park County, Wyoming," I remembered the day perfectly: "November 22, 1981." She nodded and filled in the lines on her form.

Then she asked Richard.

"Albany County, Wyoming." Looking down at me, he added, "Yesterday."

She stared at him a moment. "You were divorced yesterday and you're applying for a marriage license today?"

"Yes," he said.

"That's so sweet!" She beamed as she filled out the forms. "I knew this would happen someday. Now you just wait here while I get this notarized and filed." As she walked across the office, we heard the buzz as she repeated the story at each desk she passed: "His divorce came through yesterday and he's applying for a marriage license today—isn't that sweet?"

A QUAKER WEDDING is normally a simple affair, sans fancy dress, attendants, and elaborate rituals. The couple stands up in Meeting for Worship and speaks their vows, after which the silence of worship resumes, enfolding their commitment. At the conclusion of Worship, the clerk reads the certificate of marriage and invites all present to sign in witness.

Lack of trappings does not imply lack of thought, however. Preceding the ceremony is a deliberate and sometimes-lengthy process. A couple interested in being married applies by letter to the clerk of Meeting, who relays their request to Meeting for Business, the monthly gathering that handles business matters temporal and spiritual. If the couple's request is deemed appropriate, Meeting for Business appoints a "clearness committee" of Friends valued for their thoughtfulness and discernment to talk with the couple about their readiness for the commitment of marriage. Once Meeting has ascertained that the couple is indeed sincere and is as prepared as possible, the wedding is scheduled. Quakers say that couples marry "in the care of Monthly Meeting," conveying the belief that the worship community is a long-term partner in the relationship.

Without a nearby Friends Meeting, Richard and I organized our

own version of a Quaker wedding. We cleared ourselves by confer-
ring with the therapist we'd been seeing to sort through the issues
from our previous relationships, and talked with family and friends.
We wrote simple vows, pledging to take each other freely and equally as partners, and to love and cherish each other for the rest of our
lives. Then, on the weekend before we planned to move clear across
the country to West Virginia, where Richard had accepted a faculty
position, we invited a small group of friends and family members
to witness our ceremony, held in the yard that my housemates had
tidied up for the occasion. It was a picture-postcard-pretty morning:
the sun shone, the ever-present wind gentled to a breeze, and flowers bloomed all around. After the ceremony, my father snapped a
photo: Richard and I hold hands, our smiles positively electric, in
the midst of a cluster of friends.

Immediately afterward, we walked downtown for the civil ceremony with a local justice of the peace. When we reached his office,
though, the door was locked, the windows dark. After waiting some
minutes, I called his home from a nearby pay phone.

"He's gone fly-fishing," said his wife. "Can I help you?"

"No," I said, after a shocked pause. "I don't think so."

"What was the purpose of your appointment?"

"He was supposed to marry us," I replied, anger clipping my
words.

Back at my house, my parents and housemates were preparing
for the crowd of guests invited to our backyard reception. Friends
had already decorated our car with shaving cream and beer cans. I
tried to settle. My dad put down the spatula he'd been using to turn
hamburgers on the grill and took me aside.

"Look," he said in his quiet tenor voice. "You've done what's important; you said your vows to each other. Don't sweat the legal
stuff."

I brushed tears from my eyes and hugged him.

HUMANS ARE NOT THE ONLY species that pair for
life—and with somewhere between 40 and 50 percent of marriages
in the United States ending in divorce, we are surely not the most

successful. My favorite model from the world of other species is common ravens, the big black birds with the wedge-shaped tails and croaking voices that are the largest of North American corvids, members of the crow family. Ravens pair up for life, but every year they court each other anew, a lovely practice that humans might do well to adopt.

Courting ravens soar together on flat wings, wingtips touching, and cawing in rhythmic, percussive voices. They play, cavorting in the air. They call and chase one another, slicing the sky side by side like twin black jets; they fly loop-de-loops in the air around each other. One will suddenly fold its wings like a crumpled black leaf and somersault earthward, tumbling over and over before pulling out of the free fall at the last possible moment and flapping upward to rejoin its partner. A pair will ride a thermal high into the sky, spiraling slowly around each other on the rising columns of hot air in an aerial pas de deux, then coast downward in playful, dancelike swoops as we might ride a roller coaster.

On the ground, courting ravens often perch side-by-side, hold intimate conversations in soft raven sounds, and fondle each other's beaks. They bring each other food and build their nest together, piling up sticks into a large, untidy structure that only a raven could love. Even after the young have hatched and the raven parents are engaged in the frenetic business of foraging for food to stuff into ever-hungry mouths, raven pairs behave toward each other in an affectionate manner, as if taking time to tend their bond.

TWO DAYS AFTER OUR WEDDING, Richard and I packed up Molly and all of our belongings for the move to West Virginia. Richard slid right into the hectic schedule of a new faculty member with classes to teach, grad students to supervise, and the tenure process ahead. I set up my office in the spare bedroom of our faculty apartment, with a view of a parking lot and a twenty-story dorm. The skies were hazy, the air soft. Sirens and stereos replaced the sounds of ravens and wind. Molly got sick with a persistent fever. For weeks, her weight dropped and her temperature rose. We coaxed her to eat with special treats, measured out medicine in her favorite alligator-shaped spoon, and sang to her during middle-of-the night baths to bring her spiking temperature down. Richard and I staggered along, meeting our obligations to work and Molly as best we could, with no time for each other. Eventually, Molly recovered, but by then it was almost too late for us to recover too. By the time Molly left at the holidays to live with her mother until summer, Richard and I had to get to know each other all over again.

Richard resigned his position, and at the end of the spring semester we returned to Laramie so he could finish his dissertation in environmental economics. That too turned into a struggle. When he was close to finishing, he and his major professor clashed so profoundly about economic theory that Richard stalled. We were house-sitting for that same professor, and Richard sat at the man's desk every day trying so hard to write that sweat dripped down his face. But no words came. Finally, he abandoned both dissertation and degree. We moved to Washington State, where we lived with my brother and his family for a while. Molly stayed behind in Colorado; her mother had custody and would allow her to visit us only in summer and during the holidays. Eventually Richard and I found jobs in state government. We bought a tumbledown house in the woods and settled in.

And I took up running again. I've always loved to run. In grade school, before the passage of Title IX legislation mandated sports programs for girls, I was one of two girls granted the privilege of running with the boys in the distance races. In high school I sometimes ran practices with the boys' cross-country team, just because I loved the rhythm, the feel of pushing myself until my body flowed seemingly without effort. Running was as close as my earthbound self could come to what I imagined birds and other winged beings must feel when cupped by the air. I ran in college, striding up and down the hills near campus. After my divorce though, I quit running.

Pacing along the rural Washington roads where the air smelled like brine and algae wrack from nearby Puget Sound, I didn't time myself or aim for a particular distance. I simply strode along, legs moving, lungs working, until my body told me it was time to turn for home. On my best days, I found the cadence of breath and muscle that would carry me beyond my skin boundary and out into the golden stripes of evening sunshine, the shimmer of bumblebees laden with salmonberry pollen, the moss spangled with raindrops, and the flutelike notes of hermit thrushes echoing from high overhead. In those moments, I remembered what it was like to feel well, to trust my body, instead of resenting it for the ill health I fervently hoped I was learning how to leave behind. I had passed the five-year mark since my diagnosis. I was alive, and I believed that love was the reason.

THE BETTER I FELT, though, the harder I pushed myself. I ran longer routes. I threw myself into my job as a technical editor. At home, I cooked, cleaned, and set myself to the impossible task of clearing the jungle of blackberry vines that had taken over the small pasture next to our house. I volunteered at the food co-op and at Quaker Meeting. And I got sick—over and over again.

Each little bout would start with a persistent sore throat. That would morph into a nasty cough. Soon my muscles would ache and the lymph glands in my throat would swell into walnut-size lumps. I'd go to work until fever and chills sent me home. I'd rest, read novels, lie in hot baths, do yoga, write in my journal. As soon as I was better, I'd plunge into overwork again—and before long, I'd be sick.

I went to see our doctor. She prescribed antibiotics and decongestants; I was so desperate not to be ill that I took them. After a few nights of dreams that turned into hallucinations, I quit the drugs. Eventually, I recovered—for a while. Months later, when I went in for my annual physical, the doctor quizzed me until I confessed to my diagnosis with a connective tissue disease. That was in the past, I said, I'm over it now. She clucked her tongue and ordered blood tests.

When I came in to discuss the results, her words were eerily familiar:

"Your antinuclear antibody test gives a positive result in a speckled pattern. In other words, you've got a connective tissue disease, but I can't tell which."

She thought the regular bouts of flu-like illness were a manifestation probably triggered by stress. Since medication didn't seem to help, she recommended that I join a women's therapy group at the clinic.

"It's not that I think you're crazy," she said. "But if you can learn how to handle stress more effectively, that'll help you stay healthy."

Group therapy sounded as attractive as undressing in public to me. But when I told Richard, he saw it differently.

"You have to do something to break this cycle," he said. "It's got to be bad for you to be sick so often. I worry."

I signed up for the group.

We sat in a circle. We were instructed to listen while others were speaking, to not hog the group's time, and to comment constructively. Each participant introduced herself and talked about something that happened in her day or an issue she was working on. I let the words and emotions flow around me, until I got it: We were telling stories, spinning tales like those of myth and star lore. Only these stories were true—biased, but faithful to the teller's understanding. Our job was to sift through, recognize the themes and currents, and distill the meaning in our tales. Our stories were the medicine we could use to heal our ailing lives. "We become what we tell ourselves that we are," writes psychologist Mary Pipher in *The Shelter of Each Other*. "Good stories have the power to save us."

I didn't want to be *Susan-who-is-dying-of-a-chronic-illness*. Love had given me a chance to heal, but it couldn't teach me how to be well. I realized that I had grown dependent on being sick to give me permission to take care of myself. I didn't have the habit of being healthy. I powered through life like a car with its accelerator stuck to the floor and no brakes, slowing only when I ran out of gas. Illness had become my refuge.

The land of illness may be a useful destination of last resort, but it is not a good place to live. I could see myself becoming trapped there. So I worked at changing my habits. I practiced slowing my headlong cram-it-all-in-now pace, acting instead like someone who believed she had years of life ahead of her. I began stopping at a coffeehouse every morning on the way to work to write in my journal. I started meeting my best friend once a week for lunch, an after-work glass of wine, or a walk around a nearby lake. I persuaded Richard to get away for a weekend now and then. I did yoga and went running more regularly, and began riding my bike to work. The time between my sick bouts lengthened. I even graduated from the therapy group.

Then one of my wrists began acting up. It was tender and slightly swollen. I immediately imagined the worst: rheumatoid arthritis, like my mother. I fretted about it for several weeks and finally called the clinic. While a doctor I'd not seen before examined it, I poured out my fears, including the diagnosis with undifferentiated connective tissue disease.

He palpitated my wrist gently between his fingers. "I think you've got yourself a ganglion cyst. It's nothing to worry about. It's just a swelling of the doughnut-shaped cushion between the bones of your arm and the bones of your hand. It can happen to anyone."

He quizzed me about my daily routine. When I mentioned that I often rode my mountain bike to work, he nodded.

"That's probably it. Go easy on bike riding for a while. Wear a brace and raise your handlebars so you're not putting so much weight on your wrists."

"What about my illness?" I asked.

He ordered blood tests and scheduled another appointment.

A few weeks later, the doctor rotated my hand carefully, feeling the movement of muscle, ligament, and bone and pronounced himself pleased with the improvement. Then he pulled out the blood test results. I was anxious, unsure of what I wanted to hear.

"Everything looks good," he said. "Even your antinuclear antibody test. It's borderline, but I think we can safely regard it as negative. I'd say that you've discovered how to keep yourself healthy. Take your self-care routine as seriously as any prescription—adhere to it strictly. That's what's keeping you well."

I rushed to Richard's office to share the good news.

"I'm okay!" I said, throwing myself into his arms. "I'm okay!"

He crushed me close and then spun me in a circle, laughing out loud.

When he set me down, I told him what the doctor had said. "He thinks that I've figured out how to take care of myself, and that will keep me well."

"Oh, my love." Tears filled Richard's eyes. "I'm so proud of you!"

We took ourselves out to dinner to celebrate. As we clinked glasses and toasted, I smiled. Inside, I worried. *If the health crisis I had relied on was gone, how would I take care of myself?*

In bed later, I lay next to Richard's warm body, listening to his even breathing, and fretted. *What if the disease hadn't been real? What if the doctor who said it was all in my head had been right? Had I made up the threat of death in order to stand up for myself?*

I snuggled closer to Richard. He woke and sleepily put his arms around me. As we lay there skin-to-skin, I poured out my worries, ending with, "What if I made it all up?"

Silence stretched between us. I pulled away, anticipating rejection.

"What if?" he said at last. "If you needed to call on an illness in order to survive, you can be grateful to the part of you that managed that gift. It gave you a life to go on with."

There spoke the voice of Cancer, the dung beetle, my turning point, scavenging my shit to nurture new life. I rolled over and hugged him tightly.

He was right. If my illness was gone for good, I might never know the truth. I could live with that. The point was that I'd figured out how to live. That was the achievement worth celebrating, the story I hoped to run on.

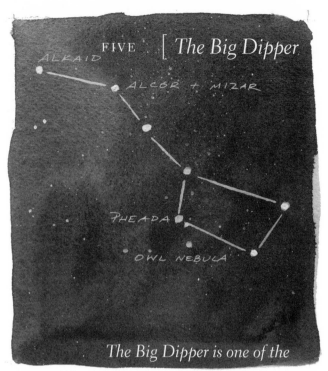

FIVE

[*The Big Dipper*

ALKAID

ALCOR + MIZAR

PHEADA

OWL NEBULA

The Big Dipper is one of the

most well-known star groupings in the northern sky. It is large,
easily recognized with its seven brightest stars arranged into a
huge ladle with a curving handle, and it is visible all night every
night over much of the Northern Hemisphere. You can chart your
course by it, and people have for millennia. The Big Dipper's
familiar outline isn't permanent, though: in a hundred thousand
years or so, it may look more like a Big Lounge Chair, as the
two stars at the end of the ladle move in the opposite direction
from the rest. Nor is it an official constellation. The astronomers
in the 1930s who laid out the constellation boundaries placed
the Big Dipper within the confines of the sprawling and lesser-
known Ursa Major, the Great Bear. (Imagine splitting up the
three-dimensional vastness of space into stellar "properties" as if
infinity were just so much real estate.)

THE SUMMER AFTER my wrist scare, we moved again. Richard was ready to finish his Ph.D. and we wanted to be nearer to Molly, so we put our house and woods in Washington up for sale and moved to a small apartment in Boulder, Colorado, just a few miles from where Molly's mother lived. Less than a year later, Richard was offered a fellowship at Iowa State University. When we broke the news of our next move to then-nine-year-old Molly, she asked if she could move to Iowa with us.

Richard and I looked at each other over her head for a long moment. How could we explain that we didn't get to decide that?

"It's up to your mom, Sweetie," Richard said gently. "She gets to make those decisions because the law gives her custody over you."

That night, Molly went home and informed her mother that she'd lived with her long enough, and now it was time to live with us.

I NEVER WANTED KIDS. When I was diagnosed, the doctors cautioned me to avoid becoming pregnant. (At the time, it was thought that the fetus and the fluctuating levels of hormones that come with pregnancy would set off the mother's immune system, endangering both lives. Pregnancy is still considered riskier for mothers with some connective tissue diseases but is no longer routinely discouraged.) It's not that I don't like kids; I simply never had any desire to take one home. My reluctance was partly because I believe that there are already too many of us on this planet and I didn't want to add my mite, and partly because I wasn't sure I had the stamina to be a parent. A character in a novel sums up my feelings. Parenting, she says, is a race where you never break the tape. It wasn't a race I wanted to run.

One afternoon a few months after Richard and I met, four-year-old Molly asked if I would be her mom.

I squirmed in my seat at my writing desk. "No." I picked my words as carefully as I picked her up for a hug. "You already have a mom. I'll be your special Suz—how's that?"

"Okay," she said, bouncing in my lap.

When Richard and I decided to get married, he consulted a lawyer. His divorce from Molly's mom was straightforward, except for custody. He wanted to share custody of Molly; Carol did not. In order to force her to share custody, we learned, we would have to prove her either mentally or physically incompetent. That seemed wrong—a battle that would likely harm Molly, no matter the outcome. Richard stewed over the dilemma for weeks and finally decided to relinquish custody. Then the man who is rarely sick went to bed for two days with a blinding pain in his head, caused, I think, by the wound to his heart. His only reprieve: Molly moved with us to West Virginia for a semester. After those four months, she spent school years with her mom and vacations with us.

Molly was eight the summer we moved to Boulder. Our first stop in the big U-Haul truck with our old Volvo station wagon in tow was to pick Molly up so she could help us apartment-hunt. We drove up to the complex where she and her mom lived, and there was Molly, perched on the fence by the entrance, watching for us as, we later learned, she had been for hours. We waved. She leapt off the fence and raced over to the truck. Richard swept her into his arms.

"Are you going to live next door?"

"No, Sweetie," Richard said, "but we won't be far away."

At first, Molly stayed with us every other weekend, then most weekends, then some weeknights as well. Then came her assertion that it was time for her to live with us.

HER MOTHER DIDN'T AGREE, but she did finally allow Molly to ride along with us in the big rental truck we drove to Iowa. Molly spent a few days helping us move into our new town house, long enough to set up and sleep in the bunk bed she and her dad had made for her in Boulder. Then we put her on a plane to Colorado.

That fall, Molly was sick frequently, and the kid who had always loved heading off to school stayed at home a lot. In our weekly phone calls, she said again and again, "I just want to live with you guys." Finally, her mom gave in and allowed Molly to spend spring semester with us. Molly loved her new school, wasn't sick a day, and immediately made friends. She also made it very clear that she did not want to go back to Colorado that summer. Neither our discussions nor Molly's desires swayed her mother, and back Molly went—and back came the weeks of missed school and finally a serious foot injury that got worse and worse until Molly was gimping around on crutches. Eventually her mother relented and agreed that after the holidays Molly could move to Iowa.

Then it was my turn to get sick, beginning with the usual flu, fever, and fatigue. I ignored it until I began having difficulty urinating. I went to the clinic and saw a young internist. He listened to my symptoms, diagnosed an infection, and prescribed Flagyl, an antimicrobial drug.

I explained my sensitivity to medications, my history of connective tissue disease, and my struggle to empty my bladder.

"Don't worry. It's just the infection. Once the medicine clears it up, you'll be fine."

After the first full day's dose, my lymph glands swelled into tight, painful knots. My pelvis ached, and my fever rose. Worse, I could now barely pee at all. I took to turning on the faucet in the hopes that the sound of running water would trigger my bladder muscles to relax; I immersed myself in warm baths; I massaged my now-tender belly. Sometimes it took me ten to twenty minutes to get a spurt of liquid out, and still my bladder would not empty. I'd get up and walk around, tell myself not to panic, sit down at my computer, write for a while, and, when I was more relaxed, try again.

Two days later, we drove to the airport in a January blizzard to meet Molly's flight. Her plane was delayed several hours by the weather, but finally there she was, ten years old, all smiles, colt-like legs, dark hair—and riding in a wheelchair.

Two days after that, my bladder quit working altogether. I slept uneasily, exhausted but awakened frequently by my distended and sore bladder. In the morning, my back and legs ached. But I couldn't pee. That afternoon, I had gone twenty-four hours since passing urine, and Richard drove me to the clinic.

The urologist on call listened intently as I told my story.

"Did you tell the internist about your difficulty in urinating?"

"I did, and he told me not to worry about it," I said. "I think the Flagyl made it worse. When I missed two doses, my bladder worked—until I took the next dose."

The doctor's face tightened. "Stop taking the Flagyl."

He thumped my kidneys, gently felt my swollen and tender abdomen, and said, "The good news is that there may not be any kidney damage. The bad news is that you're going to need a catheter for a while."

When he and the nurse inserted the thin tube into my urethra, my bladder deflated like a popped balloon. Almost two quarts of urine rushed out. I cried in relief.

"I'm going to tell you not to worry," the doctor said after adjusting the catheter, attaching the urine storage bag, and cleaning up. He grinned when he saw my face. "And I mean it. Trust me. Your bladder muscles are overstretched, but we won't be able to tell if there's any muscle damage until we remove the catheter. Worrying won't help it recover."

I walked carefully out into the waiting room, wincing as the tube pinched the walls of my urinary tract. At least my bladder doesn't hurt anymore, I thought.

Richard got up when I entered the room. "What did they say?" He took my arm.

"I'll tell you when we're outside."

As soon as we passed through the double doors, I told him about the catheter and what the urologist had said. "He was angry," I finished, "but not at me."

Richard's face twisted. He turned and punched the wall hard. "Let's get you home," he said, taking my hand.

A week later, the urologist looked me over, thumped my kidneys, probed my belly, felt my bladder muscles, and smiled.

"You scared me when you first came in," he said. "But you're much better, so I'm going to set you loose. Don't expect your bladder to perform normally just yet—be patient. The less you fuss, the faster it will recover."

I thought a moment and then decided to ask, "What happened?"

He was busy writing notes in my file. Finally he looked over. "I think it was a combination of stress and a reaction to the Flagyl."

Bladder failure in response to high levels of emotional or mental stress is not uncommon in women, he explained, "but we don't understand the mechanism."

He paused to finish writing notes and then turned back to me.

"Look, you've had a connective tissue disease, something we suspect is correlated with the body's response to excessive stress. People differ in their tolerance of stress: this bladder episode tells me that you are more than usually sensitive. Pay attention to your body. Listen to what it's telling you."

I was pretty sure what my bladder was saying: I was not ready to be a parent.

IT WAS CLEAR THAT Molly needed us—I couldn't turn away from that appeal. But it wasn't clear that I could successfully balance her needs and mine. Molly arrived to live with us near the ninth anniversary of my diagnosis. Although I had defied the initial prognosis, I was in no way confident of my ability to care for my own health while caring for Molly. I'm gender female: we tend to everyone else before tending to ourselves. Would I be able to hear my inner voice while tuned to Molly's channel? Would I find the energy to meet my needs after meeting hers?

Richard was sympathetic and assured me that Molly's arrival wouldn't change things: he would be the primary parent, if I would help. He meant that. But he's gender male: he was focused on his career, struggling to establish himself in academia at a time when faculty positions were scarce and competition was fierce. His research took him away from home about one week a month. The demands of publishing and meeting grant deadlines stretched his working hours late into the evenings. His office was on the university campus; mine was in our living room. He couldn't be tuned to Molly while being tuned to his work; I couldn't tune her out. Hence my reluctant—and swift—transition from wife of Molly's dad to Molly's stepmother.

STEPMOTHERS GET A BAD RAP in our culture. We're the cruel and uncaring women who star as villains in the stories of Cinderella and Snow White. We are portrayed as hateful, competitive, and unable to love the children we marry. Even the word itself has negative connotations. "It's colder than a stepmother's tits out there!" exclaims a character in Colleen McCullough's novel *The Ladies of Missalonghi*, and readers know just what he means.

Science isn't particularly helpful either. The theory of the selfish gene in evolutionary biology says that it is in the parents' best interest—as defined in the narrow sense of genetic survival—to go out of their way to nurture only young that bear their genetic material and to eliminate those that don't. Stepmothers aren't genetically related to our step-offspring. According to evolutionary theory, then, it is reasonable for us to behave like Cinderella's stepmother and consign our partner's children to the equivalent of sweeping out the fireplaces in return for stray crusts of bread, because the survival of their genes does not result in evolutionary "success" for us, and in fact, it may interfere with the survival of our own offspring.

Fortunately for stepchildren, altruism can trump genetics. The scientific literature is full of anecdotes of step-mothering: mother cats suckling kittens from a different litter, a sheep mother with a dead lamb persuaded to take on twins whose own mother died, elephant mothers adopting stray elephant babies. Step-mothering even extends across species: coyotes nursing abandoned domestic puppies, tiny warblers raising much larger cowbirds whose chicks supplanted their own young, humans in bird costumes nurturing endangered California condor chicks, African wild dogs nursing human children.

Still, step-mothering gets little research attention. Science has more or less ignored the phenomenon of fostering in other species, as well as step-parenting in humans. Anthropologist Sarah Blaffer Hrdy argues in *Mother Nature: A History of Mothers, Infants, and Natural Selection* that the term "biological mother" should be applied, not to the woman who provides the donor egg, but to the woman who physically and psychologically nourishes and nurtures the child. Yet never once in her exhaustive natural history of motherhood does Hrdy use the word "stepmother." It is as if we do not exist.

WHEN I WAS GROWING UP, a family that had gone through divorce was labeled a "broken home." I didn't know any real-life stepmothers; my only examples were the evil ones in fairy tales. No wonder that I felt lost and unsure of my direction in our blended family. I felt like an impostor and struggled to trust my instincts and hold my ground with Richard. Our "discussions" on parenting often turned into fights that had less to do with Molly and more to do with trust—or lack thereof. It didn't help that we came from opposing family cultures. In Richard's family, the man provided the income and the woman raised the kids and kept the household together, which for my mother-in-law meant orchestrating moves from Arkansas to Colorado to Haiti to Texas to Guyana and finally back to Arkansas, often managing four kids on her own, as my father-in-law followed his work. My parents, on the other hand, both had careers outside the home, and they shared parenting responsibilities.

ON LONG DRIVES during our family vacations, my brother and I would lie on our bunks after dark and watch the stars out the van windows, charting our direction by the wheeling constellations. You'll never be lost, our parents told us, if you can locate the North Star. Mom showed us how to find the Big Dipper and then extend an imaginary line through the two stars at the outer edge of the ladle and from there across the heavens to the bright star at the end of the handle of the Little Dipper, the North Star. Before radar, loran, GPS, and other modern technology, travelers navigated by the stars. Slaves on the Underground Railroad were instructed to "follow the drinkin' gourd" of the Big Dipper, which would lead them to freedom. Ships' navigators sighted the North Star to find their bearings in the bewildering sameness of the open sea. Immigrants crossing the hostile expanses of the Southwest's deserts on their way to jobs in *el Norte* are still guided by the North Star.

As Earth turns and orbits the sun, our view of the stars shifts: the constellations appear to proceed through the sky with the changing seasons. All except the North Star, the closest star to the celestial North Pole, the axis around which Earth revolves. Even the Big Dipper spins through the year. Yet no matter where it lies, the two stars at the end of the bowl always point to the North Star, like the needle of an unwavering celestial compass.

My brother serves as my North Star for step-parenting. His family includes three living girls, plus Anna, his first biological child, who died as a toddler. The eldest of the surviving girls, Heather, is his stepdaughter. When Bill married her mother, Heather was three years old, a year younger than Molly was when I married Richard. Heather and her sisters chart increasing degrees of biological separation: Heather and Sienna, my middle niece, share a mother; Sienna and Alice Joan, the youngest, share a dad; Alice and Heather are related only by law and the heart.

When Bill lost custody of the two older girls after his divorce from their mom, he struggled. Once he was back on his feet, both girls eventually returned to live with him. He was the quintessential nurturing parent. It was Bill who hauled himself out of bed every morning, groggy and unshaven, to cook eggs and toast bread for their breakfast, Bill who made their lunches, piling cheese and lettuce and avocado on slices of whole wheat bread. He helped the girls with their homework and attended their school activities and performances; he took them camping, backpacking, and bird-watching and, as they grew older, watched them dress up, fixed their cars, and worried when they stayed out late on dates.

When Bill began dating my sister-in-law, Lucy, then-teenaged Heather did everything she could to discourage the relationship. She didn't want to share the only dad she'd ever known, adopted, step-, or otherwise. A few years later, she and Sienna took part in Bill and Lucy's wedding. Bill cheered Heather through college and walked her down the aisle at her own wedding. When she became pregnant, Heather phoned Bill nearly every day for advice. In the photos from the hospital the morning that her son, Connor, was born, Bill is right there, cradling his first grandchild, eyes shining.

Bill's example made it plain that genetics didn't matter: what made a parent was love. That I had; I just needed to know how to apply it. I started seeing a family counselor. She suggested that Richard and I negotiate parenting guidelines, including a set of clear responsibilities for Molly: chores, bedtime, and our expectations about homework and other issues. She also recommended that we schedule time to nurture our new family, including weekly solo time for each parent, daily relationship-maintenance time for Richard and me, and one-on-one time for Molly and each of us every week.

Her suggestions made perfect sense to me. I opted for Saturday as my solo time. Richard agreed to take Molly out for brunch and then to spend the day doing Daddy-daughter things. I chose Sunday as my Molly-time. We'd go to Quaker Meeting and spend the afternoon at home while Richard went to his office. Richard and I decided to take our relationship time in the evenings after dinner. We'd walk around the block or just sit in the living room and talk about our days and discuss any issues that came up.

Reality, of course, wasn't as easy as theory. Molly hated having a regular bedtime; she whined about having to clean her room once a week and do other chores; she resented our attention to her schoolwork; she tried every means she could think of, from temper tantrums to more sophisticated dramas, to disrupt our evening "date" time. At first, her stratagems worked. As soon as Molly acted distressed, Richard folded. He couldn't bear to see her unhappy; I couldn't bear to see her manipulate him. I slid into the role of bad guy: the disciplinarian, enforcer of rules, nag, the wicked stepmother. Often it seemed like Richard and Molly were allied against me. Sometimes I felt like Molly hated me; other times I was afraid I hated her.

"You're not my mother!" she'd cry. "You can't make me do it!"

I'd take a breath, count to five, and reply as calmly as possible that while I wasn't her mother, I was, indeed, her other parent and I could most definitely make her do her homework, clean her room, pick up her dirty clothes, go to bed—whatever "it" was.

"You're mean!" she'd hurl over her shoulder as she trudged upstairs to her room. "Daddy would never make me do it!"

Ouch. *He will, if I get to him before you do,* I'd think to myself.

I kept at it, doggedly determined to be a good parent, even if that meant being unpopular. Parenting, I reminded myself frequently, was about raising healthy and stable kids, not about being liked. (Still, being liked would have been awfully nice.) About the time I began to seriously doubt my stamina and sanity, however, the emotional storm clouds would suddenly clear, and the loving and affectionate kid would emerge.

One such afternoon, Molly and I were downtown, walking to the bus stop.

"Let's skip!" she said, grabbing my hand.

"I can't skip right now, Sweet Peach. When I do, my catheter tube pinches, and it hurts."

"Can I see it? How does it work?"

"I'll show you when we get home," I said. "It's kind of a private thing. It's like a clear plastic bag strapped to my leg. There's a tube that runs into it from my bladder and a valve to empty the bag when it's full."

"Yuck!"

"Yup," I said. "Definitely yuck, but I hope I won't have to wear it forever."

"You're not going to die, are you?"

"Not this time," I gave her a hug. "But someday I will. So will you, someday. Someday's not today, though."

"Okay," she said, and held my hand all the way home.

Walks were our best time. Nearly every Sunday morning, we walked out the front door of our townhouse, headed for Quaker Meeting. We crossed the busy street hand in hand and then walked downhill through a patch of tangled woods with a meandering creek. Across the creek, we climbed uphill through a tree-shaded neighborhood at the edge of the woods and then turned left to the Meetinghouse. After the quiet respite of Meeting for Worship—the kids sat with the adults for fifteen minutes and then went to First Day School—we'd retrace our steps home.

We walked to the nearby park with its swings and slides; we walked downtown to the library and the food co-op; we walked to the university campus to meet her dad after work. Sometimes we skipped hand in hand; sometimes we walked fast to stay warm; sometimes we dawdled and counted sidewalk slabs.

We were unwittingly following in the footsteps of Henry David Thoreau. In his essay "Walking," Thoreau extols the delights of sauntering, which, he points out, "has nothing akin to taking exercise" but is in itself "the enterprise and adventure of the day." The ambles Molly and I took, although not completely without itinerary, honored the spirit of sauntering: our aim was simply to get outside and explore the world around us. We walked to experience the journey, not just to reach the destination. If arriving at a particular place by a particular time had been our only objective, we would have used the car.

Traveling on foot, we traced ant trails, sniffed ground-hugging violet blossoms, picked up autumn leaves, craned our necks to decipher the shapes of passing clouds; we watched crows jockeying for position in nighttime roost trees, followed raccoon and snake tracks, and spotted fireflies signaling in blips of green and yellow light.

Walking gave us a territory of our own, a place we could start fresh, away from the disputes that regularly rocked our household. Rambling with no agenda forced Molly and me to leave our baggage at home. Walking provided time together, and it got us outside to learn the landscape where we lived. We walked to explore, to lose ourselves and find each other in the world outside our skin boundaries.

And we grew a relationship. Over time, a funny thing happened: when Molly and I strolled arm in arm, people commented on our "resemblance." Molly, with her father's graceful height, high cheekbones, and dark hair would look down at me, half a head shorter and skinny with red-blond hair and freckles, and giggle uncontrollably. Clearly, they were seeing something not described by physical characteristics, something we couldn't see.

THE BIG DIPPER'S familiar ladle-shaped outline is traced by just seven visible stars. Binoculars reveal an eighth, the fourth-magnitude star Alcor—near Mizar, the star at the bend in the Dipper's handle. A telescope brings yet another star into view, Mizar B, a binary star that orbits Mizar. Mizar B was the first true double star discovered by telescope, most likely by the Italian astronomer Benedetto Castelli in 1617. (Double stars look like pairs in the sky: true doubles, or binary stars, rotate around each other; stars that simply appear to be paired as viewed from Earth are called optical doubles.) It took another three centuries and an instrument that sees beyond the reach of even the most powerful telescopes to show that Mizar's double is itself also a binary star, with its own companion orbiting so closely that its existence is revealed only by a spectroscope, an instrument that analyzes the light the pair releases. The view through a spectroscope also revealed that Alcor, Mizar's neighbor, is part of a binary pair. Thus the star we recognize as Mizar is actually five stars; it just takes special technology—and a close look—to see them.

When people say that Molly and I resemble each other, they're seeing beyond the surface to a kinship that originates with the love we share. We walked our way into an enduring affection. Our common ground was nature, the community of species that animate the landscapes we rambled through.

Biologist E. O. Wilson calls humans' innate empathy for other species "biophilia," an inborn bond that links humans with other life. This instinctive connection may originate in the molecules of our bodies that we hold in common with every cell of every kind of life. It is certainly reinforced by the thousands or millions of other lives we shelter, inside and out. There are ten times as many microbial cells in our body, say biologists, as human cells: the colonies of microscopic mites that preen our skin of shed cells and other detritus; the "bacterial nation" that populates our guts, a gastrointestinal consortium whose individuals digest our food in exchange for shelter from the deadly levels of oxygen in the outside air; and the organelles of our cells, which are formerly free-swimming bacteria that long ago moved in and made themselves at home, as well as indispensable.

Many of these millions are actively engaged in nurturing us. The five hundred to one thousand species and countless individual microbes that make up our gastrointestinal consortium, for instance, aid us in obtaining nutrition by breaking down carbohydrates we could not otherwise process. They also protect the environment that shelters and feeds them by fending off outbreaks of potentially dangerous species of bacteria, and they may even regulate blood flow and capillary development in our intestinal walls. These other lives interact so intimately with our existence that what we think of as "I," a solitary individual, is in reality "we," a thriving community. No wonder we have an inborn affinity for the rest of nature. It is who we are. The bonds we are born with to other species can't help but nurture our ability to link to each other.

THE YEAR MOLLY CAME to live with us, Richard accepted a faculty position at New Mexico State University and we moved to Las Cruces. Molly started middle school and quickly skipped a grade. Pretty soon she was busy with band and other school and social activities. Our walking time was gone.

When we bought a house, our new yard included a neglected and overgrown area between Molly's bedroom and the neighbor's house that was partly enclosed by high cement-block walls. I dubbed the space "Molly's courtyard" and engaged her help to renovate it. First we mapped out the sunny spots and the shade, then used string to outline new planting beds and trace a paving-stone path. Next we tore out half-dead hedges of poisonous oleander and peeled dusty ivy vines off the wall. Finally, we dug in the plants she chose: a mauve climbing rose with purple irises to shade its roots; a fast-growing native desert willow tree to fill a hot corner, where its catalpa-like flowers would attract hummingbirds; a clump of Maximilian sunflowers with their head-turning yellow blossoms; a Texas rain sage with a dense canopy of silver-gray leaves to shelter foraging whiptail lizards, flanked by salvia bushes with cherry red flowers. In the shade of a huge Arizona cypress tree, we planted her favorite wildflower, Colorado blue columbine, and slung a hammock nearby.

Eventually we completed the wall and installed a door leading directly from her bedroom to the now-private courtyard. Molly spent hours out there basking in the sun, talking on the phone, playing music, reading, studying, and napping in the shade.

Then came high school. After we all suffered through her freshman year at the crowded public high school nearby, we agreed to allow Molly to transfer to a small Quaker boarding school that seemed perfect—except that it was twelve hundred miles away and its school schedule conflicted with Richard's classes. So when fall semester at Molly's new school began, it fell to me to make the two-and-a-half-day drive to Iowa and get her settled in.

On the final evening of that very long trip, I was concentrating on threading my way through Kansas City, Missouri, at rush hour, and mentally tallying the miles yet to drive when Molly closed her book, looked over at me, and asked, "Suz, do you like my mom?"

"Hon"—I didn't take my eyes off the traffic—"I can't answer that question now. I've got to focus on driving."

"Okay," she said, her single-mindedness reminding me of her dad. "When can you answer it?"

"After we're out of the city," I said, my mind on driving.

By the time the crush of traffic had carried us down the bluffs, across the wide and muddy Missouri River, and up the bluffs on the other side of the valley, I had forgotten the question.

Molly hadn't. As soon as we passed the sign announcing the first suburb, she repeated: "Do you like my mom?"

I took a deep breath and willed my shoulders to relax. One more breath: in, hold the air, and then out.

Quakers value truth telling, even when doing so is wildly unpopular. Friends' insistence on speaking their particular truth has cost them homes, livelihoods, and families, resulted in beatings, imprisonment, and even death. The earliest Quakers refused to pay war taxes or serve in armies, convinced that killing is wrong because there is "that of God" in everyone. Friends opposed slavery in the 1700s, long before the organized abolition movement, and promoted respect for American Indians. Quakers today demonstrate against the death penalty and the war in Iraq, raise the unpopular issue of population control, and champion the rights of immigrants. I've never been imprisoned, but I have been punched, doused with tear gas, spit upon, and knocked to the ground—any of which now seemed preferable to answering Molly's question.

"Sweetie, that's a really tough question," I said, stalling for time.

"That's why I asked. You answer questions that I can't ask Dad or my mom. I want to know."

Direct hit.

Friends are keenly aware that perception of the truth is an individual thing based on our understanding of the leadings of conscience, culture, and experience, just as our perception of color depends on how our brain interprets the information from the nerve endings in the cones of our eyes. How often have you seen something you were sure is pink, only to have a friend declare it definitively orange? The truth is not just about being right; it must always be used carefully, balanced against the potential harm that revealing it may cause. The point of speaking the truth is to illuminate, not to destroy.

I didn't really like Molly's mom, but I didn't think telling that particular truth would help their often-troubled relationship. And whether I liked her mother or not wasn't the point. I needed to figure out how to answer Molly's question in a way that would be useful.

"I admire certain things about your mom. She's got a real genius for working with little kids and older folks. She appreciates them; she's creative and she really enjoys teaching—"

Molly interrupted: "But do you like her?"

I thought for a long moment. "She's not somebody I'd ever be best friends with, but I can certainly appreciate her talents."

"Hmm." And with that, she returned to her book.

After a stop for dinner with the counselor who had helped midwife our bonds, we settled in for the last leg of the drive. Molly pointed out the green lights of fireflies blinking on and off in the road shoulders as we whizzed through the darkness.

"Remember how we used to watch the fireflies in the trees outside my window at bedtime?"

"Uh-huh." I smiled at the memory.

"Am I like my mom?"

So much for warm reminiscence.

"Sweetie, I love you and I'm very tired. I have three more hours to drive."

"That's not an answer," she said.

I sighed, wishing that Richard were there to deflect her questions.

Stepparents bring unique gifts to our stepchildren. Because we are not burdened by the expectations of genetic or familial inheritance, we can love our stepkids unconditionally, just as they are. We are not troubled by fears that our stepchildren will be like us or not like us, or will turn into our parents, or that they will or won't fulfill some long-held family dream or fear. That gift comes with the responsibility to be truthful about what we can sometimes see clearly with eyes unclouded by blood or culture: the blessings and baggage inherent in their birth heritage. If stepparents lovingly and respectfully exercise the truth we see, we can help our stepchildren determine which legacies are worth carrying along and which to leave behind. That's a precious gift, and one that's as tricky to use as safely navigating a minefield.

"You're like your mom in some ways. You like doing crafts; you enjoy kids and old folks, and you're a good teacher when you want to be."

She watched me, intent.

"You take after your dad too. You've got his intelligence and intellectual curiosity, his even-temperedness, and his creativity—you're both talented at music."

"Do you like me?"

"Of course, Sweetie," I answered, taking one hand off the steering wheel to reach over and squeeze hers. "I love you too."

"Did you always like me?"

I sighed again. Truth telling is rarely easy or comfortable—especially when it means shining a light on the sides of yourself you'd rather not examine. Like parenting, though, truth telling is a form of teaching with its own potential for enlightenment on all sides.

"I love you, Sweetie," I said. "But no, I didn't always like you. I never wanted to be a mom, and at first it was difficult because I was scared that I couldn't take care of you while taking care of me. And, like all of us, sometimes you're not easy to like."

"I love you too," she said. "Sometimes I get mad at you."

"I know. Sometimes I get mad at you too. You can be mad at people and still love them. That's human."

"Good." She reached over and hugged me.

We fell silent as the car rushed through the sticky summer night, the darkness punctuated by the glowing messages of fireflies searching for their own form of love.

"Thanks for loving me," Molly said. Then she leaned back, closed her eyes, and, in the way of teenagers, fell instantly asleep.

"Thanks for walking into my life," I said softly. I wiped my eyes and drove on.

SIX [*The Pleiades*

STEROPE

TAYGETA

MAIA

ALCYONE

PLEIONE

CALEANO

ATLAS

ELECTRA

MEROPE

The Pleiades, a shimmering cluster

of stars in the constellation Taurus, the Bull, is proof that the
whole is indeed greater than the sum of its parts. None of the
individual stars in this star grouping is particularly bright,
because they lie so far away: four hundred light-years distant
from Earth. But the stars are so close together that they magnify
each other's light, forming the most well-known star cluster in
the northern sky. In Greek myth, the Pleiades were seven sisters
born to beautiful Pleione and Atlas, sentenced by Zeus to hold
the heavens on his shoulders. The grouping reminds me of my
grandmother Chris and her cluster of sisters.

Greek star lore says the sisters of the Pleiades shimmer
because they weep in mourning for the loss of a missing sister,
whose light is gone — here the stories diverge — either because she
married a mortal and left the heavens altogether, or because her
tears of homesickness for Earth doused her light.

ONE HOT SEPTEMBER evening about a year after we moved to Las Cruces, Richard, Molly, and I piled into the car, headed for Tucson to attend a memorial service for my grandmother Chris, who had died the week before after years with Alzheimer's disease.

Molly, who is prone to carsickness, took the front passenger seat and aimed the fresh-air vents at her face. As we climbed a pass in the jagged spine of a desert mountain range, the fiery ball of the sun sank below the horizon and the air began to cool.

"Do you mind if I practice?" Molly asked. "It takes my mind off my stomach."

"Of course not, Sweetie," I said.

She tugged her sheet music and flute case out of her overstuffed knapsack, carefully fitted the pieces of her flute together, lifted the instrument to her lips, and began the piece she would play for the memorial service.

Dusk blurred the angular landscape as Richard drove on, the achingly sweet notes of Molly's flute pouring out the open car windows. I hadn't cried when my mother called to say that my grandmother was dead. Now tears ran down my face. After years of drifting in a world I could not reach, my grandmother Chris, the storyteller of my childhood, was truly gone.

MY GRAN WAS TINY, petite, and slender, with fair Scottish skin, and she loved the ring and rhyme of words. In my childhood, she was chipper and cheery, as loquacious as a spring robin, always whistling an upbeat tune, singing, reciting a rhyme, or telling a story. She knew Robert Burns' poetry by heart and could deliver it in a Scottish burr, rolling her Rs and transforming her precise Vermont vowels into "bonny braw Scot." She delighted in nonsense rhymes and read to us from Robert Louis Stevenson and A. A. Milne. She sang songs about Bonnie Prince Charlie and Nessie, the monster of Loch Ness. She told tales of selchies, changelings that were seals in the ocean and humans on land, and kelpies, Scottish water witches; and of lairds and their ladies, castles, dragons, and the clans with their plaids.

Grandmother Chris' love of all things Scots came from her father, Robert G. Farquharson, a Scot who emigrated to Vermont. My gran was the middle in the brood of five girls born to his second wife, Christie Morrison. Gran always said that her father was the son of a Highland laird; in America, he was a stonemason, shaping granite into gravestones and church walls.

Once, when I was about six and helping my grandmother in the kitchen, she stopped what she was doing, took my chin in her slender, wrinkled fingers, and looked into my eyes.

"You've got rings in your eyes," she said, her voice solemn. "That makes you a kelpie. Only kelpies have ringed eyes."

She pulled me into the bathroom. "Look into the mirror."

I did, and saw the same old me: skinny, small, tousled blond hair, freckled face with a snub nose, and two eyes of indistinct hue, neither the sky blue of my mom's nor the hazel green of my dad's.

"What color are your eyes?" she demanded.

I peered at them, trying to decide. "Green?"

"Nay," she said, slipping into Scots, "they're ringed. See the starburst pattern next to your pupil? That's brown. Then right there," she said, pointing with one crooked, manicured pinkie, "See how it changes to green? And on the outside, the very edge is a distinct line of blue."

As she said it, I could see the rings in my eyes.

"You've kelpie eyes," she said. "That makes you special."

Grandmother Chris's stories were a constant background to our childhood visits. As we grew older, though, we were less interested in her world of myth and magic, and she seemed less interested in us. Her flow of tales diminished. For a while I forgot the sound of her storytelling voice.

THE WAY SCIENCE TELLS the story of the "missing" Pleiad, one star is a variable star. Its rapid rotations, about a hundred times faster than those of our sun, throw off gas clouds that cause the star's brightness to vary enormously in the course of just a few years, from the height of sparkling brilliance to barely visible. Whether tears dim its light or the star's physical instability is responsible, Pleiad only appears to vanish. No matter whether we can see it or not, it is still there.

A YEAR OR TWO AFTER Richard and I met, Alzheimer's claimed my grandmother Chris' mind, sending her to a place where she no longer recognized any of us, not even my grandfather, her husband of sixty-some years. As her memory faded, her tongue loosened. She began to talk constantly, but not to us. I strained to make sense of her soft, monotonous mutter, wanting to hear the stories I had half-forgotten. But her voice was as indecipherable to me as my face was to her. My father could make out bits of her flow of words. It sounded, he said, as if she was back in her childhood with her sisters, Jean, Dora, Marian, and Peg.

I never knew Great-aunt Jean or Marian; I met Dora and Peg only once, in separate visits when I was young. Great-aunt Dora was the plump one with the bright smile who talked a mile a minute, gesturing at the autographed black-and-white photos of movie stars that crammed her walls from her husband's career in film. I don't remember the people in the photos, but I recall clearly the careless way she adjusted her curly brown wig, which slipped askew with each expansive gesture. We visited Great-aunt Peg, my gran's baby sister, in the tidy white clapboard farmhouse in Massachusetts where she lived with my great-uncle Les and their collie, Mim. Peg was petite and slender like Grandmother Chris. I remember the enormously wide, polished planks of the floors—"pre–Revolutionary War pine," said Les with pride, and the sweet Cool Whip she served us atop homemade apple pie.

I asked my father somewhat plaintively why my grandmother had never told us stories of her sisters.

"I imagine her childhood was hard, not something she wanted to talk about."

NOT LONG AFTER MY grandmother's memorial service, I sat in the recording studio of the local public radio station with my producer as he replayed the voice tape I had just recorded for my weekly radio commentaries. Tom listened carefully to the beginning of one commentary, then stopped the reel-to-reel tape and ran it backward by hand. He played it over again, his eyebrows drawn together into a frown.

"Listen to that!" He slowed the tape, rewound it, and played it back again. "There. Do you hear it?"

"That clicking sound?"

"That's it! You're making odd mouth noises."

Tom stopped the tape, rewound it, and played a short segment once more.

"Do you know what's happening there?" he asked.

"I have no idea."

"It's weird. It's like your tongue is clicking against the side of your cheek."

"Do you want me to record these again?"

"No," he said after a moment, "it's soft enough that it won't be noticeable when I add the music bed."

He thought for a moment. "Let's change the position of the microphone next time you record. And I want you to start doing voice exercises to warm up your voice before you begin taping."

I faithfully followed Tom's suggestions: Walking to the radio station, I sang at the top of my voice — after carefully looking around to make sure there was no one nearby to hear me. I opened my mouth wide, like a rattlesnake trying to swallow a plump desert cottontail, stretching my face muscles and the hinges of my jaw. I did a practice read with the tape turned off to warm up before recording.

The odd clicking noises faded but wouldn't disappear. Tom fiddled with the angle of the microphone and changed the sound levels on the master tape. Each time I came in to record, he had another suggestion: "Take several deep breaths to relax before reading." "Try sipping water between takes." "Use plenty of lip balm so your lips don't dry out." No matter what I did or didn't do, however, the mouth noises persisted in the background of my recordings, like ghosts clapping. Tom couldn't figure them out.

"I've asked around to the other producers on the NPR net," Tom said one evening as we sat in the studio, "and no one's come across this problem before. You have a great radio voice except for those weird noises. I just don't get it."

THAT WINTER, I went in for my first physical exam since we'd left Washington State four years before. The doctor was thorough: she asked about my work, my family, and my medical history. When I mentioned my diagnosis with undifferentiated connective tissue disease twelve years earlier, she ordered a complete blood test.

One evening a few weeks later, I was lying on the couch reading a novel while Richard sat nearby, preparing his lectures, and Molly sprawled on the floor doing her homework. The phone rang. Richard answered it.

"It's the doctor," he said, handing me the receiver. I sat up. He put his arm around me.

"Susan? It's Denise. I got the blood test results. Your antinuclear antibody test came back as a strong positive. Sometimes stress can cause a false positive result, so I think we should retest in six months. But I want you to come in so we can talk."

Oh God! I thought, *It's back. I didn't make it up.* My vision grayed. The blood roared inside my head. Richard's arm tightened around me. It seemed like a long time before I found my voice.

"Okay," I said, struggling to speak even those two syllables.

"This isn't anything unexpected. And it isn't necessarily cause for alarm. Autoimmune diseases come and go, and sometimes people have positive ANA results without any illness at all. I want you to come in and talk to me."

I took a deep breath. "Okay." My voice sounded faint and distant to my ears, as if it belonged to someone else.

A few days later, I sat in her office and we discussed the test results.

"The titer of one to one hundred eighty makes it a solid positive," she said, "and the pattern of the cells is speckled. That suggests either mixed connective tissue disease, systemic lupus erythematosus, or rheumatoid arthritis."

I focused on the data: "What does the titer mean?"

"It's how many times the blood sample has to be diluted before the antinuclear antibodies don't show up. A titer of one to eighty and above is considered positive."

"I've marked these sections in the rheumatology handbook for you to read," she continued. "I'm going to consult with a colleague, but I'm leaning toward mixed connective tissue disease. Your rheumatoid factor test is negative, and you don't have significant joint degradation, so we know you don't have rheumatoid arthritis."

She said I hadn't tested positive for the antibodies correlated with lupus, either. But she couldn't be completely confident: "These diseases are very difficult to diagnose because their symptoms overlap and they really aren't well understood."

She looked over at me. "Are you okay?"

My mind had wandered. I returned my attention with what felt like a physical effort. "Yes. It's just hard to hear. I thought it was gone."

"I know," she said. "But you're a scientist. Knowing is better than not knowing."

"After you read what I've given you, we'll talk more." She stood up and gave me a hug. "Call me," she said.

At home, I waded through the medical jargon in the rheumatology handbook. The section on mixed connective tissue disease sounded uncomfortably familiar. But I thought I had learned how to be well. What had gone wrong?

Reading the technical descriptions of symptoms and indications, I realized I knew: I had wanted to be well, so I stopped paying attention, quit collecting data. The see-no-evil approach hadn't worked, however. The data I had been assiduously ignoring matched the symptoms I was now reading about.

I was not ready to recognize myself in the pages of a medical text. I wanted to close the book and forget the words. Instead, I gritted my teeth and read on, reminding myself that I needed data before I could come to any conclusion, before, in fact, I would know what the story was.

Six months later, I went back for the retest. The results were not good.

"Your antinuclear antibody test yielded an even stronger positive reading, I'm afraid." The doctor looked at me over the top of her half-glasses. "This time the titer is one to three hundred twenty, which means you're producing higher levels of the antibodies."

She took off her glasses. "How are you feeling? I mean both physically and mentally."

I carefully enumerated the litany of symptoms I had wanted to forget: the aching muscles and joints, the Raynaud's, the respiratory infections, the unpredictable fevers, the fatigue.

"But I think I'm handling it okay."

"And your emotions?"

I shrugged as tears filmed my eyes.

"Is there anything new I should know about?"

"Richard thinks I should ask you about the mouth noises."

She looked puzzled.

"If you listen carefully to my radio program, you'll hear clicking and tapping noises in the background, as if my tongue is sticking to my cheek as I speak. The noises are driving my producer nuts, and Richard wonders if they are related to my health."

"Is your mouth dry?"

"Sometimes. When I'm nervous my tongue feels clumsy."

"Do you have scratchy eyes? Do you use eyedrops frequently?"

"Yes to both."

"What about vaginal moisture—do you have to use a lubricant?"

My cheeks flushed. "Not if we're patient."

She ran her fingers gently under my jaw. "Does that hurt?"

"It's a little achy."

"Your salivary glands are slightly swollen," she said. "It looks like Sjögren's syndrome."

She explained that in Sjögren's, also called dry eye syndrome, white blood cells from the immune system attack the mucous membranes, causing them to dry out. The syndrome commonly accompanies autoimmune diseases. Mixed connective tissue disease, in fact, was once called overlap syndrome because its symptoms overlap those of Sjögren's, lupus, and rheumatoid arthritis.

"The Sjögren's symptoms would explain the mouth noises," she said. "With insufficient saliva, your tongue would stick to the sides of your mouth, making small clicking sounds as you talk. It's probably worse when you're nervous or tense. If you can learn to relax when you tape your shows, that'll help."

She looked at my file. "I want you to give up caffeine. It's known to trigger Raynaud's attacks. Removing caffeine from your diet could help alleviate the Sjögren's."

"I gave up coffee already," I protested. "I like black tea."

"Drink herb tea instead."

"I can't give up everything."

She looked at me over the top of her reading glasses. "If you want to stay healthy, find something else to indulge in."

I shut up.

She rubbed her eyes.

"I wish we knew more about this. Call me right away if you notice any changes or anything that worries you."

I THREW MYSELF INTO my writing, beginning a book on the desert where we lived. I read archeology, anthropology, and history. I waded through hydrology and water law. I burrowed into geology, botany, and zoology. I searched out journals of early explorers, pored over Spanish land grants, went to the county courthouse to examine old deeds. I found stories galore, but no matter what I wrote, the sentences came out stiff, the tales lifeless. I couldn't seem to find my writing voice.

The stories we tell come in part from the cultural baggage we collect during our long adolescence, the most protracted by far of any animal species. During those years we apprentice to our clan, absorbing habits, beliefs, behaviors, prejudices, rituals, and tastes, what evolutionary biologist Richard Dawkins christens "memes," the units of cultural transmission (just as genes are the units of biological inheritance). A meme can be a song, advertisement, style of dress, myth, family story, idea, slang expression, custom, cuisine, or anything that carries cultural knowledge. In *The Selfish Gene*, Dawkins writes that in much the same way that the molecular codes of genes pass on physical traits, the bits of information called memes pass on human culture, propagating themselves by leaping from brain to brain. Our combination of memes and genes makes each of us who we are.

I searched for my writing voice in the memes of my forebears. In my family, we don't tell stories. We are reserved and refrain from either gossip or boasting, in part due to our northern European heritage with its inherent emotional reticence, compounded by a Calvinist view of gossip and boasting as two sides of the same sin, pride. The result is a family lore as depauperate as forest on exposed granite; stories—like plants—struggle to grow from its meager soil.

What I know of my family's past comes largely from our accumulation of material culture. My great-grandmother Mira's volumes of poetry and the yellowing copies of articles she wrote for *Sunset* magazine, and my great-grandmother Jennie's landscape paintings in their vivid colors and bold brushstrokes. My grandfather Milner's collection of classical and opera records and philosophy books, carefully annotated in his fine hand. A set of Limoges china for twelve, adorned with frilled porcelain ruffles and hand-painted violets, shipped from France for some forgotten bride in my grandmother Janet's family. My grandfather Olav's black-and-white photos, developed in his own garage darkroom; the handwritten genealogy that he and my grandmother Chris traced back many generations.

After Grandmother Chris' memorial service, my mother took me to visit a whitewashed brick bungalow I had never noticed before on the edge of the University of Arizona campus. It had been built, she told me, in 1904 for my mother's grandfather Dr. William Austen Cannon after he moved his family, including my grandfather Milner, to Tucson. When Mom pulled volumes of my great-grandfather's scientific publications off her shelves, along with articles on his life, I was surprised to find a kindred spirit in the man I remember only dimly as the musty smell of woolen trousers and the shiny gold of a pocket watch.

I learned that Dr. William, as he is called in my family, was one of the early practitioners of the study of ecology, my own field in science. As I browsed his writings, I realized that we had similar interests in the workings of desert ecosystems, though he studied hot deserts the world around and I focused on the cold deserts of western North America. Like me, my great-grandfather was born in the Midwest and moved to the West as an adult. We're both late bloomers: he was thirty-two years old when he stepped off a train in the then-frontier town of Tucson in September of 1903, bearing a new Ph.D. in botany from Columbia University to begin the opportunity that shaped his career, establishing the Carnegie Institute's Desert Botanical Laboratory. I was thirty-two as well when I wrote my first book and found my writing niche.

When I discovered letters written by my great-grandfather during his tenure at the Desert Lab, I read them eagerly, hungry to learn more about this scientist in whose footsteps I unknowingly walked.

The hurried scrawl on the first few pages was oddly familiar: it looked very like my mother's crabbed script. The first letter was dated the day after he arrived, and the letters continued every day, sometimes twice a day, reporting on the progress of construction of the laboratory buildings and on his plans for research.

"I am getting impatient to get to work," he wrote not long after arriving. "There are so many things to work at that it is too bad to waste much more time. We [my great-grandmother Jennie, the painter; my granddad Milner; and his brother, George] are thoroughly in love with this country already; I am hoping to take occasional excursions to see more of it."

Dr. William's assignment was broad: to investigate the "morphology, physiology, habit, and general life-history of the species indigenous to the desert of North America." In his first year he managed to probe a dizzying number of subjects, despite often having to invent his own instruments and research techniques. He studied the anatomy of ocotillo and barrel cactus; measured the transpiration of nipple cactus, giant saguaro, creosote bush, ocotillo, and brittlebush; determined the water content of a barrel cactus; measured the diameter changes over time in saguaro and barrel cacti; and excavated the root systems of those and various other desert plants—all the while supervising the building of the laboratory complex and hosting its first team of visiting researchers. He also noted and described the multitude of Indian artifacts scattered atop Tumamoc Hill, where the lab was located; recorded the daily changes in desert weather; explored the "forests" of giant saguaro cactus around Tucson; and trekked several hundred miles north to the San Francisco Peaks to examine their very different flora.

I could see myself in his tireless and omnivorous curiosity. But where Dr. William's questioning mind led him to an illustrious career that included authoring fifty-plus academic papers and books, numbering among the founding members of the Ecological Society of America, and studying deserts in North America, Africa, and Australia, I was more easily distracted by enticing new questions. I could never focus on just one research problem for long enough to finish a graduate degree.

Dr. William wrote in a tone befitting an Edwardian scientist: cautious, dispassionate, restrained, objective. At first, my writing voice carried a similar authoritative intonation. A background in science made it easy to speak as an expert, but the results didn't satisfy me. When I turned in the first few chapters of my desert book, my editor returned them with one word in all caps scrawled atop the beginning of the manuscript: "Personalize!" What was I supposed to say?

QUAKERS FIND THEIR VOICES in silence. Friends' silent worship stems from the belief that the voice of the divine, the urgings of the spirit, can be heard only from attentive stillness. Out of the quiet comes sacred speech as individual Friends stand up and give voice to their insights. In Quaker jargon, those who speak in Meeting for Worship are "called to vocal ministry." Called, that is, by the voice of the spirit, that ineffable sacred force that impels life, and us all.

A Friend moved to ministry stands up, waits a moment for the silence to settle, and then speaks unhurriedly. The message may emerge as a poem, song, or prayer, a passage from a religious or popular book, a meditation on theology or current affairs, a personal story. After the speaker finishes, silence enfolds the group again. In Quaker practice, silence speaks.

I began to treat my work as worship, striving consciously to cultivate the inner and outer quiet necessary to hear the voice of my spirit. Once Richard left for campus and Molly biked off to school, I sat down at my computer, a mug of herb tea close at hand. For the first half hour or so, I cleared my mind by spilling its clutter of thoughts, emotions, images, and memories into an unedited, uncensored journal file, simply writing them out of my way. Then I settled in to work in the stillness I had created, ignoring the ringing of the telephone, the summons of the doorbell, the noise of cars passing on the street outside. Whenever I found myself giving in to the oh-so-urgent call of household or garden tasks, I recollected what I was about, hauled myself back to my office, wrapped the stillness around me again, and resumed writing.

I began to pay attention to the voices of life going about its business right outside my window: the soft chatter of a black-chinned hummingbird as she sipped sugar water from the feeder, the swooshing waves of desert wind passing through the Arizona cypress tree, the buzzing of digger bees quartering the ground for nest sites, the "thwip!" of buds unfurling on the jasmine vine, the mutter of distant thunder. These voices deepened my focus rather than distracting it. I started taking notes on the comings and goings of the community of our yard, just as I once had taken field notes on wild communities for my research.

At the radio station, the mouth noises in my recordings gradually waned. After one session, my producer commented that the clicks and taps were almost inaudible. "I think you're finally getting it."

On my walk home that night, I scanned the sky for stars and wondered what it was I had "gotten." Tom clearly thought he could discern a pattern in the improvement in my recordings, but I was clueless. I took a shortcut across a cotton field, relishing the escape from the glare of the streetlights, and spotted the giant figure of Orion overhead. Off to the west was the V-shaped face of Taurus, and on the bull's shoulder, the bright twinkling cluster of the Pleiades. I counted the stars I could make out in that hazy grouping and thought of my grandmother Chris and her sisters.

THE STARS THAT I LEARNED as the Pleiades figure in the lore of many cultures as siblings or close friends. Australian aborigines say that this star cluster is a group of young women; in Hindu sky lore the Pleiades are six nurses who cared for one of the sons of the god Shiva. The Onondaga of New York, the Navajo, and the Cherokee all see the Pleiades as groups of children. In Greek myth, the sisters of the Pleiades are turned into doves by the goddess Artemis and fly into the sky with Orion in pursuit. A story attributed to the Luiseño Mission Indians of Southern California has these sisters climbing into the sky to escape the attentions of the hunter and trickster Coyote.

In the story that science tells, the stars of the Pleiades, unlike most star groupings, are genuinely related, born out of a shimmering cloud of stellar dust and gas tens of millions of years ago. The brightest of the Pleiades, those visible to the naked eye, are mere children as stars go. Long-exposure photographs reveal them draped in glowing veils of bluish gas—the nebula of their origin. Fifty million years ago, that cloud of gas had not yet birthed these stars; fifty million years hence, the Pleiades as we know it will no longer exist. The brightest stars will have long since burned through their stores of hydrogen and exploded, and the cluster will have drifted apart.

My life isn't even a blink in the span of that of the stars: in the time between my birth and eventual death, the stellar cluster will appear unchanged. I will never know the Pleiades' entire story, just as I will never know the full story of my grandmother Chris and her sisters, or that of my great-grandfather Dr. William, even though their lives shaped my own. Time is an earthbound concept. The cycles of stellar birth and death happen on a far vaster scale and dimension than the scale we invented to govern our pedestrian lives. Like the natural cycles that continually rejuvenate life on Earth, the lives of the Pleiades and their stellar kin continue far beyond the future we can see or imagine.

I READ THROUGH MY JOURNAL, scanning what I had written on the days when I recorded my radio show, searching for something to explain the pattern in the mouth noises. Finally, I saw a possible correlation: on days when I failed to find my still time, when I allowed the demands of home and family to outweigh my own work, I lost my voice. I couldn't seem to still either the buzz in my brain or the clicks and taps of my tongue. But when I resisted distraction and centered myself in my work, I could hear myself and my words flowed, the truth I knew through the logical leadings of science merging with the intuitive connections of heart and spirit, like the conjunction of myth and science in the story of the Pleiades.

Our truest and most compelling writing comes from deep within, from conscious or unconscious knowledge that is innately part of who we are. For me that is the set of relationships that make up what we call nature: who sleeps with whom, who eats whom, who cooperates and who competes, and who cannot survive without whom. I know these stories both from the rigorous observation of field ecology and the experience of intimacy in my kinship with other species. I grew up in the language of science; I know its idioms and its jargon. I also grew up with myth and star lore, the archetypical tales that illuminate humanity's dimensions in words that ring and stir and rhyme. Both shape my view of the world, and my voice.

As I learned to trust my writing voice, I began to assert my needs. My first request: French doors to close the two wide archways that left my office perennially open to the rest of the house.

"They'll be expensive," said Richard.

I knew that, and once I would have yielded to frugality. But the urging of my inner voice was insistent. My intuition "knew" I needed those doors. Their ability to shut out household distractions stood for my right to a space devoted solely to my writing, a room of my own in the tradition of Virginia Woolf; their ability to transmit light and view stood for my connection to home and community. Doors would give me the privacy hear to my own voice and the stories I was beginning to discern without letting me lose sight of who and what sustained my work.

A few months later, I swung open my brand-new French doors, stopping for a moment to stroke the tight-grained wood and to thank the forests that grew it, and to admire the sparkling glass panes.

Then I walked into my office and pulled those doors shut with a solid "click."

QUAKERS DO NOT BREAK the silence of Meeting for Worship casually. When the urge to speak can no longer be denied, a Friend stands, heart pounding and palms damp, to raise her voice in the silence. The force that moves Friends to vocal ministry is, I think, the same prompting of the soul that stimulates any kind of creative work. A trembling within, a passion to communicate, urges us until we cannot refrain from speaking out, putting hands to keyboard, chisel to stone, voice to song, body to dance, paint to canvas.

My summons began with a badger.

Richard and I were driving home late one summer night after seeing Molly off at the airport when the glare of our truck headlights picked out a humped form on the pavement. I caught a glimpse of long-clawed feet, a broad back, and a white stripe bisecting a wide head as we rushed past.

"Badger!"

"Should I go back?" asked Richard.

We were both tired. But the image of that motionless shape on the pavement tugged my heart.

"Yes—please?"

He made a screaming U-turn in the two-lane highway and drove back. I hopped out, darted across the dark road, and cautiously laid a hand on the still form. The fur was warm and the body unmarred—the animal might have been asleep—but not a muscle twitched. The badger was dead. My ears tuned for approaching traffic, I slid my hands under the limp body and then hefted it with a grunt, surprised at its solid weight.

"Do you need help?" Richard called from the truck.

"No," I said, a little out of breath.

I toted the badger off the pavement, climbed down the bank below the road and walked a few yards into the darkness of the desert. When I came to a large creosote bush, I knelt and slid the body from my arms to the earth. I sat for a moment reciting a silent prayer, one finger touching the badger's dense fur. Then I brushed my hands on my jeans, trotted back across the highway, and climbed into the waiting truck.

Richard reached over and gripped my hand. We drove away into the night.

After that, I started picking up roadkill: jackrabbits, pocket gophers, coyotes, rattlesnakes, deer, and turtles. The huge porcupine, armed with a profusion of golden quills. The great-horned owl, one wing still flapping in the backwash of passing vehicles. The soft plumage of the curve-billed thrasher: its yellow eye bright, its neck broken. I touched animals that, if alive, would never have allowed my approach. My hands remember the feel of their bodies, so like mine in the stitching of muscle to bone, yet so fundamentally different.

I didn't always stop. Sometimes I didn't have time or there was too much traffic. And I felt guilty as I drove on, the form on the pavement burned in my vision.

Richard got used to my habit. He's the one who put a folding shovel in the back of the truck, who made me wear gloves if the body was mangled or bloody, who hugged me afterwards.

When people asked why I stopped, I told them that I pulled roadkill off the pavement because I hated the waste. I quoted a biologist colleague: "If you get the bodies out of harm's way, they can decompose, and the critters that feed on them don't get killed too."

It's a matter of economy, I said, like never throwing away food. Moving roadkill off the highway allows the cycle of life to continue unbroken. The materials that make up one existence can recycle into others. It was a good speech: the scientist in me was pleased. But my heart knew there was more. I didn't trust that sense, and anyway, I couldn't find words for what I felt. I kept seeing the badger: its fur sleek, its muscles solid, its body as peaceful as if in sleep—but dead.

I COME FROM A CULTURE that trusts the logical conclusions of science without question. Science has much to say about the community of the land and the interrelationships that define and sustain that community, as well as about our place in it. Ecology seems to me to be among the most reverential of the sciences. It honors all of life by listening to every voice without exception, giving words to creatures large and small, common and obscure—even those lying broken on the pavement. It chronicles the relationships that tell the great story of life as it flexes and fluctuates in its eternal dance with change, and the everyday miracle of reincarnation as the molecules from one being cycle through others from birth to death to birth, time and again. It is not the role of ecology to look for miracles or report on matters of heart and spirit. Still, reading between the lines of its data and theories, what shines out of the careful words is the presence of the sacred, demonstrated in the continuing rhythm of life as it makes a place for all of us on this green and animate planet.

WHAT MY HEART READS in the lives I haul off the highway is a parallel we have either forgotten or that we ignore: How we treat our fellow humans is directly related to, and perhaps determined by, how we treat other animals. Psychologists say that people who commit violent crimes are likely to have grown up abusing other species, setting cats afire, beating dogs, swerving to hit critters on the road. Empathy for other lives is not mere squeamishness or childish oversensitivity: it is inseparable from our care for each other. A civilized society is created as much by our private, everyday acts as it is by the laws we pass and the contracts we sign. Our personal behavior sets the model for what we expect of others.

I stop to lift mangled and battered carcasses off the pavement, moving them carefully out of harm's way, in order that life might continue its journey. For me, picking up roadkill is an act of respect and compassion. And it brings a bittersweet and unexpected gift: each body that I gather up in death touches my life with its story and the magic of its existence.

"Story is the umbilical cord between the past and the future," says writer Terry Tempest Williams. Stories nurture our connection to place and to each other. They show us where we've been and where we can go. They remind us of how to be human, how to live alongside the other lives that animate this planet. Just as Quakers believe no single person holds the whole truth, no one story can give us the whole picture. We need every voice to speak its version of truth from the silence. We need every story to guide our lives. When we lose stories, our understanding of the world is less rich, less true. Each voice lost, human or wild, erodes our knowledge of who we are.

Standing by the side of the dark highway with the badger in my hands, I understood that the clicking and tapping of my tongue was a reminder that my voice—like that of the body I held, like that of my grandmother Chris—could be stilled at any moment without warning. In the meantime, from the stillness of both mind and heart, I had stories to tell.

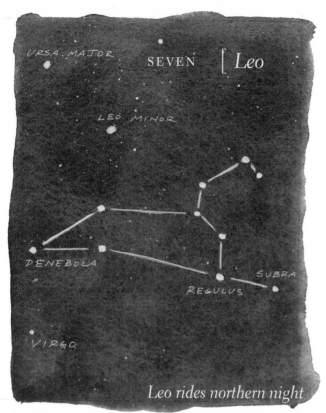

SEVEN [Leo

Leo rides northern night

skies between the sprawling form of Virgo and indistinct Cancer.
The constellation's six brightest stars trace a large reversed
question mark in the heavens that, with some imagination,
resembles the head and mane of a recumbent male lion. The
star marking the dot at the base of the question mark is Regulus,
"Little King" in Latin, a reference to the lion as king of the beasts.
This brilliant blue-white star sits directly on the ecliptic and is one
of the brightest stars in the spring sky. Looking at the constellation
through a low-power telescope, two blurry spots show up just
below the Lion's hindquarters. A high-powered scope like those
at astronomy observatories resolves these blurs into two gorgeous
spirals, each a galaxy containing hundreds of billions of stars.

113

MY DAD POSITIONED my hands on the steering wheel as the camper rolled along. "Keep us on the road," he said.

Then he stuck his head out the driver's-side window and turned his face up to the sky, binoculars in hand. Like a mirror image, my brother in the passenger seat put his upturned head out his window and scanned the heavens as well.

It was a hot day in the summer before I learned how to drive. We cruised along across a wide-open desert basin on a deserted two-lane highway, my hands on the steering wheel and my eyes on the road, my dad's foot on the accelerator, his eyes on the sky. I was perched on the engine case between the two front seats; Mom, in the dinette at the rear of the camper, was engrossed in a book. The sky was clear blue and the air rushing in the open windows was so parched I could feel it sucking the moisture from my skin.

I don't remember what species of hawk he and my brother were searching for, or even whether they spotted one. But I can still recall the feel of the steering wheel, thrumming with the vibrations of the tires on the asphalt; the sweetly turpentine-like pungence of sagebrush on the air; and the sight of the empty highway unrolling in front of us.

Joy soared through me. I felt weightless, the way I imagine their hawk might feel when a rising bubble of hot air buoys its outstretched wings, flexing feather and bone as it carries the bird upward.

I LIVED FOR SUMMER. During the school year, I searched the night sky through the branches of the locust tree out my bedroom window for Leo, my father's birth sign. As spring progressed, the stellar Lion set earlier and earlier each evening. My interest was not in my dad's astrological sign but in summer vacation. When Leo disappeared over the western horizon not long after the sun set, school would soon be out and it would be time for my family's annual summer migration.

I was born and raised in Illinois, but in my mind my real home was the West, my summer landscape, where the light was clear, the land sprawled, open and endless, inviting exploration, and sagebrush perfumed the dry air. The West was sun-ripened apricots warm and sweet off a tree; it was ice-cold soda pop at the end of a dusty hike; it was bison hooves drumming in the night and lightning bolts shooting out of clear blue sky. It was mountain ranges as mysterious as those of any fairy-tale castle, black night skies studded with a treasure trove of stars, the rising sun tinting distant peaks rose-pink. I read and daydreamed my way through the school year. In summer, I lifted my nose out of the books and came alive, happy to follow my family's summer itinerary wherever it led, as long as that was west.

My dad's wanderlust set us on the road each summer. Born and raised in the lakes and hills of northern New Jersey, he headed west for the first time in 1950 after graduating from college, driving a 1937 Ford sedan. His aim: Berkeley and graduate school. At the University of California, he fell in love with my mom and the outdoors. His half-Norwegian, half-Scottish thrift meant cheap dates. They went on hikes and picnics, saw UC football games, and explored free public parks and beaches. He planned to camp at Mount Lassen on their honeymoon, but the snow was too deep that June. They stayed in a lodge instead and picnicked on a deserted park road, smiling at the camera beneath rooftop-high white drifts. Our family trips were shaped by Dad's thrift and his delight in discovering nature. We hunted for rocks and seashells, identified wildflowers and wildlife, and, when he became hooked on birds, chased new species.

One winter when we were in Florida visiting Grandmother Chris and Grandfather Olav, Dad decided it was time to teach me how to use binoculars. We were watching scrub jays when he put the strap of his heavy binoculars over my head.

"Spot the bird with your eye, first." He pointed to an azure blue and tan jay, perched on a nearby branch. "Then hold your head still and bring the binoculars up to your eyes, like this." Guiding my hands, he brought his binocular lenses up to the pink frames of my smudged glasses.

"Can you see it?"

"No."

"Let's try again. Are you looking right at it?"

I nodded.

"Keep looking at it and hold the binoculars to your eyes."

I gripped the heavy glasses tightly in my small hands.

"Can you see it?"

"Yes!" I said as the jay leaped into my field of view, larger than I could have imagined. Startled, I moved and the bird disappeared. "I lost it!"

"That's okay," he said. "Try again."

After I mastered binoculars, Dad taught me how to look for field marks, distinctive characteristics that identify the different species: feather color and pattern, beak shape, flight configuration, behavior, habitat. I enjoyed watching birds, but I never developed his fascination for all things winged and feathered. That fell to my brother. Bill took to bird-watching like a religious calling: he read bird guides at night by flashlight under the covers, the way I devoured novels.

ON THAT HOT DAY in the sagebrush basin when my dad turned the steering wheel over to me while he and my brother craned their necks to the sky, they were looking for a species of hawk they had not seen before. My dad could spot a bird when it was just a dark speck in the sky. He had great eyes.

Until glaucoma. Three years after Richard, Molly, and I moved to Las Cruces, my then sixty-five-year-old dad abruptly lost the peripheral vision in both eyes and part of the central vision in one eye. His glaucoma was not a surprise—he had known about it since I was in college and had faithfully been taking the medications recommended by his doctors, who believed it was under control. His vision loss came suddenly, out of the blue.

Glaucoma can be a sneak thief, stealing eyesight with little warning. In the most common form, the meshlike drain that allows excess intraocular fluid to escape from the inner eye becomes blocked in a process that some researchers think may be similar to the clogging of arteries in heart disease. The resultant increase in fluid pressure squeezes the optic nerve, the bundle of fibers that connect the retina with the brain, carrying the information we interpret as images. Over time, the slow strangulation caused by high ocular fluid pressure damages individual fibers in the nerve bundle, resulting in fewer signals transmitted and thus, less sight. Once damaged, the nerves never regenerate. Most forms of the disease lack symptoms, giving sufferers no warning that their ocular nerves are diminishing. The ocular fluid pressure can be controlled; the loss of sight is irreversible.

LONG BEFORE HE WAS diagnosed with glaucoma, my dad progressed from watching to studying birds. A friend who had a license to band birds had invited my father to assist him, and my dad was captured as surely as the birds in his friend's mist nets. (Bird banders place numbered metal rings on individual birds' legs. Recapturing banded birds gives researchers a rare window on their lives, revealing daily and seasonal movements, population changes, and migration and habitat needs.) My dad's hands, so used to the beaker and flask of a chemistry lab, proved equally dexterous at cradling the warm, feathered bodies of birds. His mind, trained in the precision and patience necessary to create and test new pharmaceutical compounds, was perfectly suited to collecting and analyzing banding data. Bird banding allowed him to get closer to the feathered objects of his interest and to contribute to science.

One September weekend not long after my dad began banding, my parents and I drove to northern Minnesota to visit Hawk Ridge, a linear feature that parallels Lake Superior, offering an aerial lift to hawks migrating along its shore. Every fall, a group of bird banders set up shop on the rocky crest to net and band passing hawks.

When we arrived, the activity was already in full swing. Several people stood near the nets, ready to untangle and subdue trapped hawks. Once in hand, each bird was processed in a scientific assembly line from the scales to gauge its weight and the ruler to measure its dimensions to the pliers with which to attach the numbered ring to the hawk's leg. People called out weights and measurements, band numbers, and species names to the tabulator. I watched in fascination. Soon someone passed me a hawk to hold.

Hawks do not submit graciously to being handled. After removal from the net, each struggling bird's wings were folded against its body by the bander, and the hawk slid headfirst into a can with both ends removed. Immobilized by that metal straightjacket, the bird could safely be held. Small hawks like American kestrels and merlins went into tennis ball cans, the head with fierce eyes and sharp beak sticking out one end, the graceful tail out the other. Bigger species went into two- or three-quart-size cans taped together end to end.

I watched as banders removed a red-tailed hawk from the net. Its wings stretched almost as long, tip to tip, as I was tall. When that redtail in its metal tube was handed to me, I was surprised by how light the huge bird was. It seemed insubstantial for its size, as if made of air, not muscle and bone, synapse and feather.

Bird bones are, in truth, partly air. Like the framework of an airplane, a bird skeleton needs to be light enough to enable the bird to stay airborne, and strong enough to withstand the enormous stresses of choppy air currents. (Airplane designers have long borrowed ideas from bird skeletons.) Unlike rigid airplane structures, though, bird's skeletons must also power their flight, adding a whole new set of engineering issues. Birds save weight and retain flexibility without sacrificing strength by pneumatization, a lovely word that sounds like what it means: pumping air into something, in this case the hollow interiors of their bones. In many species, the bird's skeleton weighs less than the feathers that cover it, thanks to those air-filled bones. The redtail I passed along weighed in at just two and three-quarter pounds, less than the arm that held it.

Birds breathe the air into their bones. When a bird inhales, the air rushes into inflatable sacs in the back part of its body and, from there, into the cavities inside its bones. On exhalation, the breath pours from the bones into the bird's lungs, where oxygen migrates across cell membranes and into its bloodstream. From the lungs, the air flows into the frontal air sacs, another chance for oxygen diffusion, then exits the bird's throat. This two-stage respiration not only allows a bird to lighten its skeleton by literally filling it with air but also to be very efficient in harvesting the oxygen from each breath—hence some species' ability to dive deeply and stay underwater for long periods without breathing, and others' ability to fly at altitudes as high as 30,000 feet, far higher than where we humans gasp for breath and ultimately expire.

The skeletons of different species of birds show different degrees of pneumatization, depending on their aeronautic needs: diving birds such as loons and auklets possess the most solid bones and are, by and large, poor flyers; hawks and others that spend much of their lives riding the streams of wind have the airiest bone structures.

Their hollow innards make bird bones ideal for musical instruments. The variation in the strutlike internal structures that strengthen these airy bones results in characteristic sounds produced by the bones of different species. Some birds bones sound eerily like the living species' own calls. Ceremonial eagle-bone whistles blown by the Hopi and other Indians of the American Southwest sound very like the huge birds' screams, while turkey wing bones sounded by hunters in the Southeast emulate the plaintive calls of hens.

Flying, birds play the air. The air also plays them.

WATCHING MY DAD BAND, I understood why he was captivated: holding a bird is about as close as we earthbound humans get to feeling feathered flight. When Molly was ten, we spent Christmas with my parents in Tucson. One morning, my dad opened his mist nets in the backyard and took Molly out to help him band. He showed her how to untangle each bird from the strands of the net and how to hold it without injury, cradling it gently on its back in her hand with its head sticking out between her middle and index fingers, her thumb and other two fingers lightly pinning its wings. After they had weighed, measured, and determined the sex of a bird and then banded it, he let Molly release it. She cupped winged wildness in her hand for a moment, stroking the silky smoothness of its plumage and feeling the rapid patter of its heartbeat before opening her fingers and freeing the bird to fly away.

A few years later, my dad began having trouble seeing the birds in his nets. His eye doctor tested Dad's vision and reported no problems. Months later, looking at his computer monitor, Dad realized that he couldn't see the entire screen. When he closed one eye, part of the screen vanished. His eye doctor rushed him to a glaucoma specialist. That doctor confirmed Dad's worst fears: he was losing his eyesight.

The specialist tried laser surgery. He burned holes in the drain in each of Dad's eyes to improve fluid drainage and relieve the damaging pressure. After the surgery, Dad's intraocular pressure dropped for a while, then crept up. He went in for a second round. This time, Dad's pressure bounced right back to the danger zone. And he continued to lose vision.

Undaunted, Dad went to see another glaucoma specialist, who cut a new drain in his left eye, the most damaged one. While that eye was healing, Dad lost more sight. Before he could have the same surgery on his right eye, his health maintenance organization dropped that specialist. So Dad found a new doctor. This one diagnosed low-tension glaucoma, a little-known form of the disease in which nerve deterioration occurs under what is otherwise considered normal eye fluid pressure. After this specialist cut a new drain in Dad's right eye, the pressure in both eyes dropped significantly, and his vision loss slowed. Still, his seventieth birthday gift was losing his driver's license.

THE SPIRAL GALAXIES in Leo are ordinary, except for their behavior, which appears to violate Newton's law of attraction. They are rotating so fast that astronomers cannot explain why they haven't spun apart or how the space between them can be filled with searing-hot gas. Either Newton's law of attraction is wrong or the universe contains an enormous amount of mass we cannot see. Astronomers generally favor the second possibility, speculating that perhaps 90 percent of celestial material is invisible "dark matter," ranging in size from subatomic particles to brown dwarf stars and black holes. If we could see this invisible material, familiar celestial sights like our own Milky Way, and the two perfect spiral galaxies in Leo, would appear ten times larger. What we see in the heavens may be less complete than we think—like the view through my father's eyes.

AFTER LOSING ABOUT 60 percent of his vision, my Dad is now considered legally blind. He still studies birds, though he has retired his nets and banding pliers. These days, he works at his specially modified computer, compiling data that he and other researchers have collected and readying it for publication in journals and on the Internet. He can no longer see the computer keys well, so after nearly sixty years of hunt-and-peck, he is teaching himself to touch-type. He reads laboriously with the powerful magnifying lenses of a jeweler's headset or with a special scanning monitor. My mother often reads longer articles aloud to him, and then he goes over the details himself, word by enlarged word.

He still watches birds too, though he can no longer drive to birding hot spots, and the feathered forms he could once spot easily at great distances are now visible only nearby. After some experimentation, Dad realized that one eye is better for perceiving distant objects, the other for details. So he employs his two eyes independently, forgoing the binocular vision that characterizes our species, in order to use his remaining ocular nerves efficiently. He and my mom still hike, but now they ride public buses to area parks and greenbelts or take a van with a hiking group from their senior center. And they still travel, though mostly with family whose eyes they can depend on.

After a trip to South America, Dad reported that he'd gotten great views of an Andean condor.

"Wow!" I said. "That's really cool."

"They have ten-foot wingspans," he said with a grin. "That makes them big enough for me to see."

I didn't know whether to laugh or cry.

When I think about my Dad's steady good humor in the face of losing the sense we rely on most, I am reminded that Regulus, the brightest star in his constellation of Leo, is also called Cor Leonis, "Heart of the Lion." That's my dad.

WHILE MY FATHER was losing his vision, I was losing my breath. The respiratory infections that had plagued me when we lived in Washington State returned with a vengeance one especially dry year in Las Cruces. Whenever the desert winds filled the air with clouds of dust and pollen, turned the normally blue skies hazy brown, my sinuses and lungs filled with crud. Simply breathing became an effort. I quit running. I tried inhaling steam at night and sleeping with my head elevated. I even resorted to drugs. Nothing helped lift the fog of fatigue.

That spring, Richard achieved the dream that had sustained him through graduate school, the writing of two dissertations, and our many moves: he was granted tenure, a professorship for life. We went out to dinner to celebrate, and he was ecstatic, almost giddy. I was happy for him but couldn't quite match his joy.

The next morning I rose at dawn to make a cup of tea in the quiet before Molly and Richard woke. Standing at the sliding glass door, I looked over the backyard wall at the familiar bony silhouette of the Organ Mountains. The rising sun tinted their rocky slopes delicate pink, the sky was hazy blue, and the faintest hint of green tinted the desert landscape.

"This is home now," I said out loud. "We're here for good." I remembered the red-tailed hawk I'd held so long ago, its wings pinned inside that straightjacket of cans, its heart beating wildly. My breath caught in my throat. I felt like weeping.

In the twelve years since we had driven away from Wyoming's sagebrush-scented plains, I had tried to love each place we had landed: West Virginia and its dark hollows, the rainy woods of Washington State, the sweeping rise of the Rocky Mountains in Colorado, Iowa's gentle hills, and now, this spare desert. And all along, I had secretly hoped that fate and the academic job market would somehow return us home. When Richard was offered the position at New Mexico State University, I saw Las Cruces as my best chance to settle in the West, even if the sunburnt Chihuahuan Desert was a long way from the Rockies and sagebrush.

When it came time to house-hunt in advance of our move, Richard was off at professional meetings and Molly was on vacation with her mom, so I piled our houseplants into our Volkswagen bus and set out across the middle of the continent. Several days of record-breaking June heat later, I parked at the summit of the Organ Mountains above Las Cruces, climbed a spiny ridge, and looked over a landscape colored in a thousand shades of dry. Everything I could see shimmered, the hard lines of rock and pavement wavering in the midday heat. A lizard rested, panting in the thin shade of a nearby shrub. A tall dust devil whirled and skipped across a bare farm field in the valley far below. I inhaled a great lungful of searingly dry air.

Here is a spacious landscape, I thought. And my inner voice wailed: *It's so brown! And so hot!*

That night, alone in my motel room, I cried myself to sleep.

ONCE WE WERE SETTLED, I set out to make the desert home. I learned the geology of the skinny, angular mountain ranges alternating with wide, dusty basins, the ecology of life in what writer Mary Austin calls "the land of little rain," and the stories of the humans who have inhabited this dry and often difficult place. I steeped myself in desert lore and experiences, on the assumption that familiarity and facts would breed connection. I came to love the desert for its spectacular contrasts and sudden magic, for the creativity shown by all the lives that call it home. But no matter my resolve or my efforts—how much I learned, or how many stories I wrote—I never quite felt at home.

For some people, home is definite and specific: a family, a town, a neighborhood, or a building. For others it is a particular place or landscape, perhaps the region of their birth or upbringing, or some other place that tugs heart and soul. Even if we cannot name home, we can often describe how it smells, as if our bond comes from a place more elemental than words. Like the ability to read cues in a man's scent signature that reveal his fitness as a mate, our sense of home may arise from factors crucial to our well-being that we cannot consciously perceive, much less measure.

I had a vague sense that my respiratory problems were a symptom of something the desert did not provide, some critical element without which I failed to thrive the way plants growing in soil that lacks iron sicken and turn yellow. Certainly, the desert air lacked the fragrances of the landscapes I call home: the turpentine-like pungence of sagebrush washed by spring rain, the resinous odor of sun-warmed pine sap, the musky scent of rutting elk, the vital dampness of a dawn muffled in new snow. But I couldn't prove that those smells, or their chemical components, were critical to my connection to any particular place. Nor could I explain, much less quantify, why their absence so affected me. One cannot eat them, wear them, pay the mortgage with them, or save them in a college fund. Staring out the sliding glass door at that view of dawn-washed desert peaks, I told myself that homesickness was a weakness. I could get over it.

"FOR SOME PEOPLE," writes Barry Lopez in *Arctic Dreams*, "what they are is not finished at the skin, but continues with the reach of the senses out into the land. . . . Such people are connected to the land as if by luminous fibers, and they live in a kind of time that is not of the moment, but in concert with memory, extensive, measured by a lifetime. To cut these fibers causes not only pain but a sense of dislocation."

I get my luminous fibers from my mom, who was born and raised in the fog zone that edges San Francisco Bay. Her definition of "mountain" is the glacier-polished granitic architecture of the Sierra Nevada where she hiked and camped in her youth, her feel for sea cliff, wave form, and beach sand was honed on the central California coast, her affinity for desert shaped by visits to her grandparents in Tucson. She learned to appreciate the Midwest in the more than thirty years that she and my dad lived there, but her heart remained firmly fixed in the West. It was her yearnings that aimed our summer vacations westward and that settled my parents in Tucson when they retired. No wonder that Bill and I headed West as soon as we could: my brother is rooted in the coastal forests of the Pacific Northwest; I belong to the arid spaces where sagebrush grows, mountains define at least one horizon, and stars fill clear night skies.

Homesickness may not be a diagnosable illness, but it is more than mere sentiment. The word itself, writes Carolyn Servid in *Of Landscape and Longing*, allows the truth that when we are away from the places that nurture heart and spirit we feel "unhealthy, ill at ease." Americans are a restless culture, moving constantly in search of new opportunities, which we define in terms of money, possessions, and power, not the richness of connection. If we valued roots—attachment to place and the community of species that live there over material success, we might well be happier, less driven to accumulate things and more able to be nourished by what we have and who we love. The malaise that captures us when we live in a place or culture that nurtures neither heart nor spirit may be telling us that we, like ET, need to honor the call to go home.

The rising sun poured heat through the glass and I shivered as I looked out at the desert. I wanted with all my heart to go home, but Richard's tenure award meant we were fixed, at least until he retired. And that time was decades away. I wrapped my arms around my chest for warmth and walked into the kitchen to make my tea.

LATE THAT SPRING, our doctor examined my throat and nasal passages, felt my lymph glands, and listened to my lungs. "I think you've got respiratory allergies."

Great. "I have mixed connective tissue disease, Raynaud's, and Sjögren's. Isn't that enough?"

"This isn't about fairness. It's about trying to figure out what's wrong. Being sick all the time wears you down and makes your underlying illness worse. You need to see an allergist."

I grunted.

"I know this is hard," she said, "and I'm sympathetic. But I'm serious. You need to find out what's going on."

She shut my folder. "Is there anything else we need to talk about?"

"No." Homesickness was a state of mind, not an illness.

"Talk to Richard about the allergy tests," she said.

I did, and he agreed with her. "I hate to see you so sick. I worry."

Ouch. The thought of explaining yet again about my health and the unconventional choices I'd made to manage it was exhausting. But I hated the thought of worrying him.

"Okay."

He put his arms around me. "Do you want me to go with you?"

I took a deep breath and sat up straight.

"No, I should be able to handle it on my own."

"'Should' has nothing to do with it. If you want me there, I'll be there."

I brushed away tears. "No. I'm a big girl. I can handle it."

At the allergy clinic, the doctor skimmed the multipage questionnaire I'd labored over, listened to my breathing, and pronounced his diagnosis: chronic rhinitis, or respiratory allergies. He pronounced testing to be the first step. Once his lab staff had identified what substances I was allergic to, he explained as he wrote in my file, he would make up a dilute preparation of allergens, and a technician would inoculate me with them twice a week. "Continuing exposure essentially trains your immune system to tolerate the allergens and decreases the allergic reaction."

"I'm concerned that the allergy shots might degrade my overall health," I said.

"The allergens are administered in extremely low doses. Most people experience no problems."

"I'm not most people," I said, reminding him that I had been diagnosed with an autoimmune disease. "How long would I have to take the shots?"

"Some people become accustomed after a matter of months. Others need them weekly for several years."

I stared at him, shocked.

"Years? But couldn't the long-term exposure damage my immune system?"

He looked at his watch, finished writing, and stood up. "The laboratory staff will schedule you for your first testing appointment," he said, and walked out.

I talked it over with Richard. He thought testing was a good idea. He suggested discussing it with our doctor.

"I'd go ahead with the allergy tests," she said. "You need to know what's causing your respiratory distress. We can decide about treatment after we get the results."

I called the allergy lab and scheduled the tests.

The lab technician drew a three-column-by-seven-row grid on my left bicep with Magic Marker. Each square, she explained, would be injected with a different allergen preparation, except for the first three, which were control solutions.

"I'll inject three at a time, and then we'll wait fifteen minutes for a reaction. I'll grade the swelling, record the results, then inject you with the next set."

I didn't react to any of the household substances in the first session. At the next, however, we hit pay dirt. As soon as she injected one particular solution of plant pollens, my nerve endings burned. The skin inside that Magic-Marker-delineated square quickly swelled into a lump that distorted the grid's parallel lines like a funhouse mirror.

"Weed Mix Number 6," said the technician cheerfully. "Looks like a good reaction."

While I waited through the rest of the injections, I read the list of plants included in Weed Mix Number 6: tumbleweed, kochia (pronounced KOH-shuh), and pigweed, all plants that spread their highly allergenic pollen far and wide on the desert winds, all true weeds that had hitched rides to the desert from distant lands. Like me, they weren't native to the place, but unlike me, they had taken so successfully to their adopted home that they flourished throughout the landscape. There was no escaping them.

I trudged home, my arm throbbing. Two blocks away, I stopped to rest. The lump had ballooned, making it look like I'd been pumping iron one-armed. That bicep was hot to the touch. At home, I slid onto the couch.

When Richard returned from classes, he was impressed.

"Which was it?"

"Tumbleweed, pigweed, and kochia. They're everywhere."

"You're allergic to this place."

"Yup."

"I love you."

I reviewed the test results with our doctor. She had consulted with specialists; they counseled against the allergy shots. We discussed other treatment options, none of which seemed attractive. She wrote a note in my chart and then looked at me.

"What do you want to do?"

"Go home to the Rockies." I said without thinking. When the words left my mouth, I felt a rush of air as when a hawk flaps its wings.

"Didn't Richard just get tenure?"

"Yes."

WHEN RICHARD ASKED what I wanted for my birthday that September, I answered without hesitation, "A weekend in Salida."

Salida, a small town in the mountains of south-central Colorado 510 miles north of Las Cruces, was Richard's home for part of his childhood. In Cabe family memory, Salida is the halcyon place where the sun always shines and the sky is blue, and they are picnicking in the mountains on Chalk Creek, square dancing in the Scout Hut, sledding on the golf course, or shuffling up the buffalo at the talent show before the matinee at the movie theater. Richard was barely a year old when my father-in-law's job as a mining company purchasing agent moved the family to Salida; four years later, the mine closed and the company transferred them to Haiti. More than fifty years later, my sister-in-law still remembers crying her heart out as my mother-in-law drove them away down the winding river canyon.

Richard introduced me to Salida the summer we married. I was charmed by the high, sagebrush-scented valley ringed with snow-flecked peaks and the small town with century-old brick houses, their wide porches overlooking tree-shaded streets. After that we visited almost every year, going out of our way to pass through that particular corner of rural Colorado. We'd stop for a few hours or stay overnight to walk the neighborhoods, noticing houses for sale. We'd wander the historic downtown, sit by the river as the sun set, and gawk at the blizzard of stars that lit up the night sky. And we'd dream about living there. Reality always intruded, though, the reality of making a living in a two-stoplight town that, charm and scenery aside, lay two hours from the nearest university, city, major airport, and interstate highway.

One June, we headed north to Denver for a business trip and, as always, took the long route so we could spend a night in Salida on the way. It was dusk by the time we reached the mountains, and Molly, who had just gotten her license, was driving. I sat in the front seat beside her with my eyes closed and my nose flared, sucking in thirsty gulps of the cool, fresh air streaming in the vents. I was searching for the turpentiney fragrance of home—sagebrush—but what trickled in was another familiar smell, sweet as licorice with an overtone of wet spring earth.

"Wild irises!" shouted Molly, swerving onto the shoulder and coming to a jerky stop by the side of the highway.

"Look, Suz! The wild irises are blooming. We're home!"

My eyes popped open, and I piled out of the car, stiff from so many hours of driving. The three of us stood arms around each other in the chill air. Below the highway, hundreds of pale blue Rocky Mountain iris blossoms floated above the verdant green grass of a mountain meadow, shimmering in a perfumed mist in the dusk.

When I asked for the birthday trip, I didn't tell Richard what I'd told our doctor. My practical self knew a move was impossible. Still, I hoped a few days' visit to Salida might help. Like tuberculosis patients sent west for "altitude therapy" in the belief that the region's thin, dry air would heal their lungs, I imagined Salida's air could restore my breath—at least temporarily.

EACH TIME WE DRAW a breath, we inhale our surroundings. "Deep in the lungs our bodies become continuous with the atmosphere," writes biologist Robin Wall Kimmerer in *Gathering Moss*. "For better or worse." Although our skin is the largest surface of our body in constant contact with the air, she says, it is in our lungs that the relationship becomes intimate. The oxygen molecules we inhale migrate into our blood, and from there through our entire circulatory system, eventually reaching every cell in our bodies. With each exhalation, the atmosphere takes on characteristics of us as well, flavored by our waste gases.

We inspire more than oxygen. Air is laden with freight, including other gases, some of which, like carbon monoxide, are poisonous; airborne chemical compounds, both natural and synthetic; lives such as microscopic yeast and algae spores and plant pollen; particulates from industrial chimneys and vehicle tailpipes; soil particles; and all manner of other minute detritus. Some of what the air carries is global, dispersed around the world on high-altitude winds; some is local, originating within a few miles or feet. Each lungful of air is unique, a blend characteristic of the place where it is inhaled.

Breathing, we reaffirm our link to the rest of nature, especially with Earth's plants and other photosynthesizing lives, our "breathing-buddies." We and these green beings respire in a lovely symmetry: they exhale the oxygen we need, we exhale the carbon dioxide they need. Breath merges our separate lives, infusing our cells with the elements common to all life.

ON OUR LAST MORNING of that weekend trip, we walked to the edge of town and admired the view of peaks crisp against blue sky. I inhaled lungs full of cool, pungent air and joy bubbled through me. I twirled in two great giddy circles, my arms thrown wide for balance, and skipped.

Richard was staring at me.

"Sorry," I slowed to a walk.

"Don't stop. It's been a long time since I've seen you skip."

"It's the place," I said. "It fills my spirit. I feel like I could fly."

That afternoon, we began the long drive back to Las Cruces, winding up and over a mountain pass and then descending through silver-green expanses of sagebrush into increasingly drier and sparser shrublands.

As the desert's hazy smudge appeared on the horizon, my nasal passages swelled up. I began to pant through my mouth. A tear trailed down my cheek.

"What's wrong?" Richard took a hand off the steering wheel to lay it over mine.

I took a wheezing breath.

"I don't want to go back. I've tried to make the desert home, but it's not. I can't breathe there. I miss the smell of sagebrush and wild irises, the crunch of snow, the view of the stars. I miss home!"

I put my face in my hands and wept.

Richard pulled to the side of the highway, reached into his back pocket, and handed me his handkerchief.

I wiped my face. "I'm sorry. I know it's unreasonable, but I just want to go home."

He held my hand. "Would Salida work?"

I stared at him, hardly daring to hope.

"If that's what you want, my sweetheart," he said, "we'll figure out a way. I don't know how we'll manage it, but we'll do it. I promise we'll bring you home."

A few weeks later, we made an offer on a historic but quite dilapidated brick duplex near downtown Salida. The place was not my dream: the windowpanes were cracked, ceilings sagged, the wiring needed replacing, plants grew through a gap in the floor, the roof leaked, and the yard was landscaped with discarded tires and car batteries. But it was what we could afford. We figured we could make it habitable and rent one side, while keeping the other for summer visits and sabbaticals. Our friends thought we were crazy. I pinned a photograph of the little brick structure, sagging porch and all, to the bulletin board in my office. It reminded me of a Quaker saying: "If you follow the leadings of your heart, way will open."

I didn't go back to the allergy clinic. Months later, I received a letter from the doctor reiterating his diagnosis, his assessment of the seriousness of my condition, and his prescription: allergy shots twice a week for the foreseeable future.

"If you do not follow our recommendations," the letter warned, "we cannot be held responsible for your health."

I laughed. He didn't get it: he wasn't responsible for my health. I didn't need allergy shots. I simply needed to follow my heart home. How, I couldn't yet see, but I had faith: way would open.

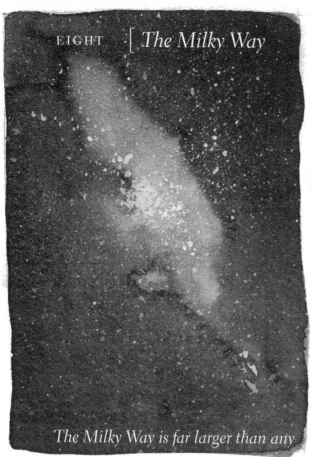

The Milky Way is far larger than any

constellation: it spans the heavens from horizon to horizon.
Viewed on moonless nights away from city sky glow, this band
of stars pours across the sky like a moonlit river. The stories of
astronomy say that this sparkling stellar swath is the flattened-
wheel shape of our own galaxy. From our perspective two-thirds
of the way out from the galaxy's center, the more-distant stars
form the milky belt across the sky, while the closer ones resolve as
the groupings we call constellations. In the tales of mythology,
the Milky Way is a celestial river, the source of all life, or a path
connecting this life to the next, this world to what lies beyond.

ONE FEBRUARY MORNING during Molly's first year of college, Richard and I rose before dawn to catch a flight to Portland, Oregon, to visit her. As we drove across the desert outside Las Cruces headed for the airport, glimmers of day began to lighten the sky in the east, but the Milky Way still poured its stellar flow across the sky.

Seeing the Milky Way is one of my measures of landscape fitness: if I scan the sky at night and can spot that glimpse into the far reaches of our stellar neighborhood, the place is healthy. Unfortunately, light pollution has erased the once-ordinary view of our galaxy in most cities and urban areas. According to the National Oceanic and Atmospheric Administration, more than 80 percent of Americans live where the Milky Way is no longer visible, and fewer than half of us have ever seen heaven's river of stars at all.

I grew up watching the Milky Way pour across the night sky. When my brother—bursting to share the skills he was learning in kindergarten—taught me how to count, I practiced on the stars in the Milky Way. I remember lying on my back in my sleeping bag, chanting silently: "One, two, three, four. . . ." I fell asleep before I ran out of numbers and drifted into dreams inspired by that stellar stream.

Each new landscape that Richard, Molly, and I moved to after leaving Laramie's dark skies had more light pollution and fewer stars. Las Cruces was among the worst, with its pervasive orange haze of streetlights. I missed seeing the Milky Way curving across the heavens like a luminous bookmark, a stellar reminder of our place in the vastness of outer space.

A FEW WEEKS AFTER we returned from that weekend visit to Molly, Richard and I sat in our backyard one night. He was talking about his consulting work, which involved testifying in cases around the country related to competition in the rapidly diversifying telecommunications industry, while I searched the sky glow for the season's celestial phenomenon: Comet Hale-Bopp, approaching Earth on its swing from the outer reaches of the Milky Way. I knew Richard loved the challenge of being an expert witness; I also knew he was so busy with that work he was having a hard time keeping up with teaching his classes.

"I'm due for a sabbatical," he said. "But I'm inclined to apply for a year off instead, so I can continue the expert witness work. I can do that from anywhere that has decent access to an airport. We could spend the year in Salida."

I stared at him, open-mouthed.

He was quiet for a moment.

"In fact, if the work holds out, we might be able to stay in Salida."

Every morning, I looked at the photo of our dilapidated duplex pinned to my bulletin board, the image reminding me to have faith and way would open. Now Richard, always logical, never one to leap before carefully analyzing the situation, was suggesting that way might open decades sooner than I had dared to dream.

He took my hand. "You've moved from place to place for my work. Now it's your turn. If Salida is where you want to be, that's where we'll go."

I swallowed and found my voice. "Really?"

"I want you to be happy. I want to see you skipping when you walk."

A month later, we set out for Salida to interview a contractor about renovating the duplex. It was long past sunset by the time we neared the end of our nine-hour drive. Richard was driving as I dozed.

"Suz," Richard said suddenly, pointing to the black sky over the peaks. "Look!"

I woke, blinked, and looked. A brilliant silver spot danced in the heavens, pulsing like a beating heart and shadowed by a vaporous tail: Comet Hale-Bopp.

He reached for my hand. "It's pointing to Salida."

Just then, a shooting star arced across the sky and fizzed out right above the highway in front of us.

"Two positive signs," he said. "We're going home."

AFTER MOLLY ARRIVED HOME from college that summer, we packed our household into the largest truck we could rent and moved to Salida. The contractor had planned to be finished renovating the duplex by the time we arrived, but in the way of all construction projects, the work had taken longer and cost more. We camped in a motel for a week and then moved into a construction zone permeated by the whine of power tools and punctuated by a parade of carpenters, plumbers, painters, and other crews.

Richard's expert witness work kept him on the road. He'd often arrive home from the airport Friday night, spend the weekend in his office writing testimony, and depart Sunday afternoon. I unpacked our household, transferred bank accounts and other affairs, helped Molly settle in, kept tabs on the renovation, and attempted to find my writing rhythm.

I looked forward to our wedding anniversary that August. Richard promised he would take the day off so we could spend some rare "couple" time together. On the two-hour drive through the mountains to pick him up at the airport, I belted out the blues along with Bonnie Raitt. When I arrived, I learned that severe weather had rerouted his flight. Four hours later, Richard disembarked from the bus that had carried him the last leg of his journey. He looked exhausted. After we hugged, he told me that a new case had come up and he would have to work through the weekend. Then he nodded off while I drove home. I was lonely and overwhelmed from trying to hold our household together. I reminded myself that his work had made our move to Salida possible. Unreasonable as it might be, I needed our day. Surely he could spare time to celebrate our anniversary?

The next morning, after I made his breakfast, unpacked his suitcase, started the laundry, and saw Molly off to work, I got mad.

"Your work has always come first. That hurts me."

"I have a deadline. I'm working hard so that we can live here. I don't know what else you want me to do."

"I just want some of your time. I didn't marry you for your income—I married you for your company."

"I'm doing the best I can!" He hurled over his shoulder as he stomped next door to his office.

I laid my head on my desk and cried. This was not the homecoming I had imagined.

ASTRONOMERS SAY THAT what we call the Milky Way is simply our view of our own galaxy, a whirling wheel measuring 100,000 light-years across and 2,000 light-years thick. (For those who are inclined to calculate the size of the chunk of celestial real estate occupied by our galaxy, a light-year is about six trillion miles.) The estimated one trillion stars that make up the galaxy form a wheel with a hub at the center and two arms spiraling out from either side, curved by the galaxy's spinning motion as it hurtles through space. Around the hub is a region of blazing light where the density of stars is a million times that of our celestial neighborhood; here stars are created, flare, and die in massive explosions. In its heart lies a black hole, where gravity sucks in everything, even light, as if the galaxy were continually swallowing itself.

Richard and I talked through our differences that day, but when he left the next afternoon, the loneliness and feeling of being overwhelmed returned. My days were consumed with keeping tabs on Molly, keeping up with the construction crews, keeping our household functioning, and keeping up with writing deadlines. I felt like a black hole was consuming the joy I had expected to find in moving to Salida. And I wondered when the light would return.

In his journal, Quaker George Fox recounts a haunting vision that came to him when he despaired of ever finding the spiritual path he sought for so long. Fox writes that when he cried out to God asking why he had to suffer through such misery, "I saw . . . that there was an ocean of darkness and death, but an infinite ocean of light and love, which flowed over the ocean of darkness."

MY OWN OCEAN OF LIGHT, it turned out, lay quite nearby. Although we loved our neighborhood next to downtown, with the Arkansas River flowing by just two blocks away, and we reveled in rarely needing to start our car because we could walk to almost everything we needed, including hikes into the hills across the river, we needed more space. Even after the renovation project was complete, our duplex, while charming, was cramped at just over 1,500 square feet for the three of us, two home offices, and our perennially energetic Shar-Pei, Dida. Most importantly, there was no room for a studio where Richard could set up his wood- and stone-working machinery. He wanted a shop building, so while he traveled, I walked through town looking for a suitable property. I finally found one—right next door.

Thus, barely a month after our anniversary we became the proud owners of Richard's dream shop building, located on the neighborhood eyesore, the abandoned half-block of former industrial property across the alley from our duplex. What we half-jokingly labeled our "decaying industrial empire" included enough land to someday build our own house, plus a crumbling century-old brick shop building. The shop's once-ornamental brick parapets were missing bricks, its chimneys in disrepair, its tin roof leaked in a dozen places, and inside, it was dark and filthy. But it boasted twice the floor space as our entire duplex, giving Richard plenty of space.

The half-block of property itself was not exactly charming: littered with rusted industrial junk, some identifiable and some not, carpeted with a knee-high growth of weeds, and surrounded by six-foot-high, chain-link fence topped with sagging barbed wire. But it offered views of the peaks over the roofs of town. And it included a block of frontage on Ditch Creek, a thread of spring-fed waterway that slips through downtown Salida.

I HAVE ALWAYS WANTED a creek to play with. This one, though, was in as bad shape as the property it bordered. Channelized to accommodate a railroad line in the late 1800s and later dredged for flood control, its shallow flow ran ruler-straight between bare banks colonized by invasive weeds and littered with chunks of concrete, asphalt, and other industrial debris. Undaunted, we promptly "adopted" the block of neglected waterway after consultation with the city, which owned the opposite bank. As we hauled away trash, I assessed what we had undertaken.

I started with the plants. Reading the patterns they draw on the landscape reveals the ecological history and possibilities of a place. The story they told was daunting: kochia, one of my desert nemeses, grew in abundance on our new creek bank. This scraggly, pyramid-shaped, red-stemmed annual weed is an invader native to arid central Asia that succeeds all too well in the American Southwest. Kochia can rapidly take over disturbed soils by gambling on speedy and abundant reproduction. When conditions are good (plenty of soil moisture and daytime heat), kochia seeds sprout, blanketing the ground and crowding out seedlings of competing species. Then they commandeer available water and nutrients, spring upward, sprout masses of tiny flowers that loose abundant and highly allergenic pollen into the air, and seed profusely. As soon as environmental conditions deteriorate, kochia plants dry up and vanish, leaving behind bare soil and bumper crops of seeds that persist for decades, ready to sprout a carpet of fuzzy infant plants as soon as conditions turn favorable again.

Our industrialized creek bank had become kochia heaven, with a sprinkling of other invasive weeds including tumbleweed, Siberian elm, and cheatgrass. Restoration clearly would not be simple or speedy.

SO RICHARD AND I SET TO WORK. We spent evenings and weekends weeding—and weeding, and weeding, filling our utility trailer with prickly kochia carcasses. It was hot, hard work. But it brought sweet rewards.

One afternoon, we uncovered our first native plants: two small clumps of streambank willow. The stems, clearly lopped repeatedly by the prison crews that "maintained" the creek for the city, were just a few inches high. Still, they could jump-start our restoration project. Protected from weed whackers, each clump would quickly shoot up four- to five-foot-tall, wandlike stems. As the roots spread, new stems sprouting from their nodes, the willows' diffuse canopy would shade the creek, cooling the water and shrinking the algae mats that choked its flow, and shedding a steady rain of nutrients to feed baby trout, caddis fly and mayfly larvae, and other aquatic inhabitants. The willow thickets would eventually cover the bank, discouraging the sun-loving weeds, enriching the impoverished soil, and creating habitat for native bunchgrasses and wildflowers.

I talked to the city public works director. He agreed to tell the crews to spare the plants we marked. We bought a roll of fluorescent pink flagging and wound it on stakes next to the two willow clumps.

Inspired, I imagined the entire ecosystem reweaving itself, beginning with the microbes that live in the pores between the grains of earth, the sticky threads of fungi that bind soil particles against erosion and exchange water and nutrients with plant roots, and the microscopic arthropods that roam about in the soil, eating and being eaten. The overstory of grasses, wildflowers, and shrubs that shade the surface and add their organic litter as mulch and compost. The ants, spiders, and insects crawling, flying, pollinating flowers, grazing leaves, and distributing seeds. And the larger lives, swimming, burrowing, or flying overhead.

I couldn't buy microbes, fungi, insects, birds, snakes, mammals, and native fish. They would have to return on their own. But I could encourage their homecoming and give our pioneering willow clumps company by planting more kinds of native shrubs, the natural overstory along our high-desert creek.

I pored over nursery catalogs, searching for species that would grow in the moist soil next to the water, species that would thrive on the hot and dry upper bank, species that would attract butterflies and other pollinators, and species that would provide berries for fruit-eaters. I considered shape, texture, fragrance, and color at different seasons. Then I calculated the size of my budget and trimmed my choices.

In the end, my list came down to seven: red-twig dogwood for the wet soil next to the creek, where its scarlet stems and white berries would stand out in winter; golden currant and skunkbush sumac to bloom as winter eased into spring; Indian plum and chokecherry for nectar-bearing summer flowers and clusters of edible fruit; rubber rabbitbrush to color the upper bank with golden late-summer blossoms; and big sagebrush for its evergreen canopy and characteristic fragrance.

I ordered as many "tublings," several-inch-tall shrub starts as we could afford. And then Richard and I went to work with pick and shovel, prying holes in the hard-packed soil and hauling water bucket by bucket. The sprigs were invisible at first, buried in the weeds, but I visited them every week, drinking in the fresh oxygen they respired, exhaling puffs of my own carbon dioxide to fuel their growth.

NOT LONG AFTER we planted our first set of baby shrubs, Richard took a day off to climb one of the summits visible from his shop, 12,051-foot-high Simmons Peak. We packed knapsacks and lunch, strapped hiking packs on Dida, and drove to the trailhead. We followed a trail up through the forest to the high saddle between Simmons and a neighboring peak. From there, we'd go cross-country and angle our way up Simmons' rocky face.

We ate lunch at the saddle, with its panoramic view of our valley far below. From that height, the towns and roads shrunk to miniature size, and the wild reaches of rocky canyons, rumpled hills, and high peaks took over. The sun warmed our skin; a breeze swished through the clusters of bristlecone pines; Steller's jays and Clark's nutcrackers called as they flew past. Dida strained at her leash, eager to follow enticing smells.

After eating, we hiked up a steep ridge and began to ascend the peak itself, traversing a wide boulder-choked avalanche chute on the way to a rocky rib that led to the summit. Richard crossed the steep talus steadily; I moved hesitantly, gripping Dida's leash tightly, well aware that one missed step could start a pinwheeling free fall to the cirque far below. Whenever my eyes strayed to the dizzying drop, my vision grayed and the boulders under me seemed to sway.

Each hop from rock to rock brought a fresh wave of vertigo. Finally, I sat down atop a large boulder, tears leaking from my eyes. Richard hurried back.

"What's wrong?"

"I can't do it," I wiped my eyes. "When I look down, the ground spins. I feel like I'm going to fall."

He pointed to a rib of rock protruding from the far edge of the boulder chute. "If I take Dida, can you make it that far?"

I nodded and passed him Dida's leash. Then I scuttled on hands and knees from rock to rock in an undignified crawl.

Finally I reached a patch of alpine turf with a solid rock wall at my back. The earth steadied.

"How's your breathing?"

I stared at Richard.

"You think it's my lungs, that I'm getting vertigo because I'm not pulling in enough oxygen. That's a horrible possibility."

He nodded. "I'm sorry, my love."

I took a shaky breath.

"You go ahead," I said. "I'll wait here."

He kissed me and scrambled up the ridge, headed for the peak.

I sat in the embrace of turf and ridge, one arm around the dog, my knees drawn up under my waterproof parka for warmth. In a lifetime of hiking and some rock climbing, I had never before failed to reach a summit. Dida licked my face as tears trickled down my cheeks.

When Richard returned, he took Dida's leash and we headed slowly back across the avalanche chute.

On the hike downhill, I was quiet. My thoughts kept returning to that bout of vertigo. I suspected that Richard was right: the dizziness was a sign of a symptom I had been warned about but had hoped to never know, decreased lung function. If my lungs were indeed impaired and absorbing less oxygen, what were my chances of life in Salida, at seven thousand feet above sea level? I didn't want to imagine.

THAT WINTER, an American dipper, the same species known from pristine mountain streams that had serenaded Sadie and me as we left on our Thorofare journey, practiced its warbling songs in the culvert at the upstream end of our block of Ditch

Creek. The next spring, a muskrat dug a burrow in one bank. A red fox investigated the creek bank on its predawn hunting rounds. By the end of the second summer, we could spot our young shrubs above the weed canopy, and the two clumps of willow had formed a small thicket. Other natives were beginning to return too: Indian ricegrass with its airy cloud of seed heads, neon-bright scarlet globe mallow, sand dropseed grass, drifts of purple fleabane.

A nattily dressed older man often stopped to talk when we were out weeding the creek bank and carrying water to our shrub sprouts. Joe was a neighborhood fixture: technically homeless, he slept and showered in the basement of the Presbyterian Church across the street. In return, he did handyman work for the church. When he wasn't fixing something there, Joe could be found feeding squirrels in a nearby park, picking up stale baked goods from the grocery store to restock his squirrel-feeding supplies, or watching the news in the hospital waiting room across town. He also listened to voices no one else could hear and recorded their teachings in neat cursive in the notebook he carried in his breast pocket.

One day Joe stopped by Richard's shop to ask if we had a place where he could park the shopping cart he used to store his tubs of squirrel food. In return, he said, he would keep an eye on our property and the construction of the new house.

We talked over Joe's request at dinner that night. He might be crazy, we decided, but he'd never done anything more harmful than offend people with his eccentric theology. And he was our neighbor. So we agreed to let him use the old tin pump shed that sat on the creek bank just below where stubby sections of rebar protruded from foundation walls marking the outline of our house-to-be.

A few days later, Richard helped Joe slide open the heavy, rusted door on the tin shed. The inside was empty but for greasy residue from when it had held control valves regulating the flow of crude oil from tanker cars on the railroad that had once run across the creek to aboveground tanks that had stood where our house was now taking shape. I brought Joe a pail, rags, and a broom, and he spent the rest of the day cleaning out the shed. Over the next week, he dragged in several shopping-cart loads of belongings. Soon he had the shed all fixed up with a card table, tidy stacks of plastic tubs labeled with the date he had filled them, a clothespole, and plastic crates containing other neatly arranged supplies.

Joe spent every day at the pump shed, refreshing the contents of his squirrel-food tubs, sitting in the sun and writing in his notebook, and tending a feral cat he had adopted. Whenever I was out weeding or watering, he came over to talk. He'd ask me to point out the "good" plants, cite statistics he had written down about whatever national issue troubled him at the moment, or assure me that when the world ended and the chosen few started over, Richard and I would be among them. Sometimes I avoided him so that I could weed in peace.

Once the new house plumbing was in, Joe asked for a hose so he could help water. A few weeks later, he snagged me to identify some wild plants that had sprouted on a dusty bit of bare creek bank he'd been faithfully watering.

"Are they good?"

I dutifully looked and was surprised to see a patch of Rocky Mountain bee plant, a native wildflower I had been hoping would appear as we restored the creek's plant community. The seeds had apparently survived through all that had been done to the place, and Joe's gift of regular water had awakened them. Each bee plant stem sprouted green leaflets, arranged like fingers of a hand, and spikes of tight pink buds that would eventually open into starry flowers with long stamens dancing in the breeze like golden hairs.

When the wildflowers I called Joe's bee plants bloomed, swallowtail butterflies—the first we'd seen on the property—arrived by ones and twos as if summoned out of the air. They fluttered around the flower spikes, hovering to sip nectar from the small pink blossoms.

One afternoon, a black tiger swallowtail fluttered past my head almost close enough to touch on its way to drink at Joe's patch of bee plant. I admired its elegant midnight-black wings, edged with rows of bright yellow dots and the neat black tails on each hind wing. The butterfly hovered and sipped, and then fluttered toward another native plant that had sprouted nearby, dragon wormwood, a relative of sagebrush with leaves that smell like tarragon. When the swallowtail reached the wormwood, it danced in the air around the plant, hovering to stroke the fragrant leaves with its antennae and legs as if making love, or laying eggs. (Later, I checked in my butterfly book, and sure enough, it—she—was likely laying eggs. Dragon wormwood is the main food of this swallowtail's caterpillars.)

We were out weeding the creek bank on a chill and breezy morning the following spring when Richard discovered a newly emerged adult black tiger swallowtail on the ground near the dragon wormwood plant. The butterfly's jet-black wings were still wet and crumpled from the chrysalis. Richard propped up a piece of wood to shelter the insect from the breeze and we watched as it clung there in the sunlight, pumping life into the wad of tissue that slowly became shimmering wings. Eventually the butterfly fluttered off, marking the first generation of swallowtails to hatch from our reawakening creek.

WHILE WE WERE COAXING our block of Ditch Creek back to life, Richard's father's life was gradually ebbing. His downhill slide began with pneumonia and complications the year after we planted those first shrubs. After lung surgery, Mr. Raymond came home tethered to a supplemental oxygen supply. My father-in-law never recovered. Each year when we visited Arkansas, he tired a little more easily and shed a little more weight; over time, his skin faded from healthy pink to nearly gray. The year that Dida died and we adopted a Great Dane, Isis, Mr. Raymond was hospitalized several more times.

His doctors eventually diagnosed terminal pulmonary fibrosis, a lung disease caused by repeated exposure to fine particulates like the dust in the mines and milling facilities where he had worked, as well as by some autoimmune diseases. Richard's dad left the hospital to come home into hospice care. So Richard and I, along with Isis, began driving the thousand-mile commute to Arkansas each month to help with his care.

At first, we simply kept Mr. Raymond company, freeing my mother-in-law to drive to the store, get her hair done, or play an afternoon of bridge. We'd park Isis' enormous dog bed in an out-of-the way corner of the family room and make ourselves useful. Richard's dad fussed at us, impatient with the tether of his oxygen hose and asserting that he would "get better" soon.

But as he progressed from being able to walk the length of the house, carefully maneuvering the oxygen hose around obstacles, to needing to sit down and rest midway along, to being unable to walk farther than the bathroom, his focus shifted from fretting about the tasks he could no longer accomplish to remembering the past. He began quizzing Richard about Salida, recalling friends, associates, and businesses he had known fifty years before. For the first time in Richard's life, he and the father who had despaired that his dreamy, artistic middle son would never come to anything useful shared a mutual interest.

During one visit, Molly flew in from her home in Portland to join us. She had taken her grandmother out to do the grocery shopping and I was perched on the fireplace hearth near where Isis snored, when Mr. Raymond folded up the section of newspaper he had been reading, aligning the corners of each page perfectly, and asked about my lungs.

"I'm okay, as long as I don't try to climb peaks."

"You don't do well with medicines, do you?"

I shook my head, surprised that my father-in-law would know that detail. We generally stuck to talking about the weather, gardening, Molly's accomplishments, or Isis, of whom he had grown quite fond. He twitched the hose of his oxygen tank until it lay in a perfect S curve on the carpet. "I hope you never have to use one of these things."

"Me too."

He drew in two wheezing breaths.

"I hope you never feel this bad."

Richard, who had come in on the end of our conversation, walked over and laid his hand on his dad's shoulder.

His father turned to him. "Do you all do your banking at First State? That's where we banked."

"No, dad, it's not there anymore."

A few minutes later, Mr. Raymond looked his watch. "Where are Alice and Molly? They should be back by now."

"I think they went to Wal-Mart, Dad. You know how long that can take."

"I don't believe I've ever been to that Wal-Mart. What'd they do, drive all the way to Denver?"

Richard looked puzzled. I whispered in his ear: "He thinks we're in Salida."

BY OUR NEXT TRIP, my father-in-law was bedridden. Richard helped his dad eat and helped him sort out his medications. He learned to change his dad's diapers. He calmed my father-in-law when he woke disoriented. And he answered question after question about Salida, the place where his father increasingly lived in his mind.

We had been home from that trip less than twenty-four hours when we got the news that Mr. Raymond had taken a turn for the worse and was refusing food and water. We repacked our bags, loaded Isis in the car, and lit out late the next afternoon.

It was nearly midnight by the time we crossed the dark landscape of the Texas Panhandle on a lightly traveled two-lane highway. I peered out the windshield at the heavens.

"Wow!" So many stars crowded the sky that I could barely pick out the constellations.

Richard slowed the car and parked on the verge of the deserted road. We got out and stood for a few minutes with arms wrapped around each other, heads tilted to the sky. The Milky Way stretched from horizon to horizon like a wide band of silver cloud.

"On a night like this," I said, "you can see why so many cultures have seen the Milky Way as a connection between this world and the next. It looks like the trail that souls would follow on their final journey."

"I wonder if my father will live through the night," Richard said.

RICHARD'S FATHER DID LIVE through that night. But when we arrived at the family home, we were surprised at how much his condition had deteriorated: his body had shrunk so that his skull dominated his face; his skin seemed almost transparent. Still, he recognized us, saluting with his trademark two-fingered wave when we walked in the bedroom door to join Richard's three siblings and my mother-in-law.

Richard leaned over and grasped his dad's upraised hand: "We're here, Dad."

His father smiled.

Later that night, I sat with my father-in-law as he dozed. "We promised we'd be back," I told him softly. "Now all of your kids are gathered around you."

His hand twitched convulsively, plucking at the afghan that covered his emaciated legs.

I reached for his fingers: "It's okay to let go; we'll take good care of Miss Alice."

His hand clenched once and then relaxed. He slept.

THE NEXT MORNING, my father-in-law greeted us by waving and reaching for our hands. He seemed more alert. He even roused himself to say "Bow-wow-wow!" when Isis poked her huge snout into the room. By midmorning, though, Mr. Raymond was agitated and no longer responsive. He stared through us without recognizing our faces.

That night we kept vigil at his bedside, "midwifing his dying," in Richard's words. My mother-in-law held one of his hands, Richard kept one arm around her and one hand on his father's shoulder; my father-in-law's favorite caregiver held his other hand; I sat at the foot of the bed, one hand on his feet and one arm around Richard's eldest brother. My father-in-law's breathing grew shallower and more labored, with increasing space between breaths until finally his chest simply didn't rise again.

The caregiver felt his pulse. "He's gone."

The room was silent except for the chugging of the oxygen compressor.

My mother-in-law began to sob. Richard comforted his mother; my brother-in-law went to call the hospice nurse; I switched off the oxygen machine.

Later, I slipped outside. The Milky Way glimmered faintly

through the orange glare of the streetlights overhead. Richard came out the door and wrapped his arms around me.

"There he goes," I said, pointing to the trail of stars.

We stood holding each other, sending our love to help Richard's father on his final journey.

Looking up at the stars, I thought about the seedlings we had planted on our creek bank, visualizing their roots growing deep and their branches spreading wide, inviting the return of the community of the land: the microbes, fungi, insects and other arthropods, reptiles, amphibians, birds, fish, mammals, humans included, and the interrelationships between those lives that keep the landscape healthy. Planting those shrubs was an act of faith, like having kids, a gift to a world we likely wouldn't know. Life might be very different by the time our creek bank was once more a flourishing ecosystem, but we were operating on the conviction that the shrubs and their descendants would thrive, carrying our love for the place into a future we wouldn't see.

By entering into life, we take on the certainty of death as well; the grace of existence emerges from that continuing tension. That same tension lies at the core of our galaxy, where the black hole that can suck in and destroy immense stars apparently recycles them, spewing out streams of super-high-energy particles and radiation that will eventually seed new galaxies. What we leave behind as tangible evidence of our time on Earth are the molecules that once constituted us and now, liberated, cycle through birth and death and birth again in the ongoing pulse of existence.

By helping Richard tend his father and working to restore the creek-side community whose respiration would sustain all of us, I was restoring my own life's rhythm, rooting myself in a place I call home.

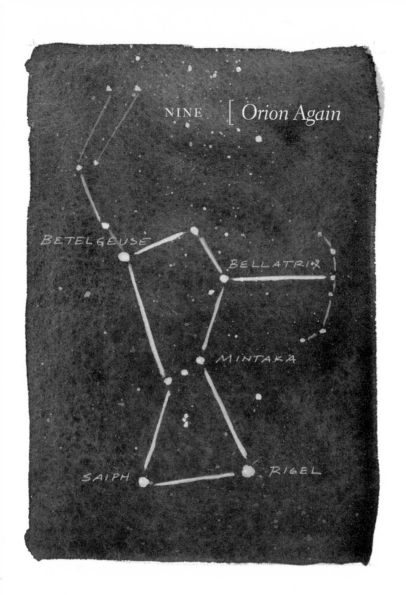

BETELGEUSE

BELLATRIX

MINTAKA

SAIPH

RIGEL

IT IS FEBRUARY. I wake, as I usually do, in the half-dark on the cusp of the day. I snuggle close to Richard's warm body and drowse until I hear a squealing yawn: Isis. When I open my eyes, I can just make out two triangular Great Dane ears turned in my direction like huge antennae and the gleam of two large brown eyes. She is curled up on her dog bed, waiting for her humans to get up. My day has begun.

I kiss Richard, haul myself out of bed, pull up the blind, and look at the sky. Orion has long since set over the peaks that trace the western horizon. Jupiter shines bright in the eastern sky, and the waning quarter-moon sails toward the west.

I squat to pet Isis and check her nose—dry and warm, not a good sign for a dog—and her bed, dry also, which is a good sign for an aging Dane whose capacious bladder does not always make it through the night. I ruffle her ears and head for the kitchen to get her treats. She follows my progress with ears perked but does not get up. When I return, treats in hand, she gulps them delicately, then sighs gustily and lowers her head to her bed when Richard and I unroll our yoga mats.

I've been greeting the day with yoga and prayer for more than two decades. (And for that whole time, even though I know my yoga routine is good for me, I've had to talk myself into doing it every morning.) After we moved into our new house last summer, Richard joined me in this dawn ritual. Facing east, toward the sunrise yet to come, I begin with gentle stretching asanas, working the sleep-stiffness from my body. I hold each pose for a few breaths, counting inhalations and exhalations by silently reciting the cardinal directions: East, where the sun rises. South, where the light comes from. West, where the sun sets. North, where the cold comes from. Then Mother Earth, Father Sky, Community of the Land, Self. For each repetition, I visualize our landscape: the ridges of the Arkansas Hills across the river to the east, the mass of Methodist Mountain rising to the south, to the west the pyramid-shaped peak of Mount Antero in the Sawatch Range, to the north the double-humped summit of Buffalo Peaks. I add the rocky earth underfoot, the heavens overhead, all of the diverse lives whose interrelationships make up this place, and last, myself, right at home.

When I have finished stretching and saluting the place where I live and my place in it, I rise to my knees. Extending my arms toward the dawn, I imagine myself traveling the globe from east to west with the sun and greeting friends and family along the way, bringing their faces and places to mind as I send them love and blessings.

As the sky grows light, I rise, both feet firmly planted on the floor, and ground myself for Salute to the Sun, a sequence of yoga poses that give thanks for the day. I inhale and stretch upward, reaching for the heavens to lengthen my spine and release its tension, and then exhale and bend forward, stretching to the earth, relaxing my lower back and opening my pelvis. Poised between earth and sky, I move from one pose to the next in an undulating rhythm, doing my best to integrate movement and attention with breath.

Breathing in, I focus inward, listening to the stretching and singing of my muscles, ligaments, and nerve fibers; feeling the strength of my bones, hearing the pulsing of my blood and the respiration of my cells, as well as the voices of those legions of other beings that inhabit the ecosystem I call my body. Breathing out, I reach out, focusing my awareness on the world beyond my skin boundary: Isis on her bed, Richard on his mat, cars passing on the street, deer hooves in the garden, geese calling as they fly overhead. As I link inner and outer worlds in the rhythm of breath and movement, the earth turns, bringing the new day.

I finish with a prayer to the spirit that animates all life, asking to see and appreciate the beauty around me, to listen carefully for the voice of the sacred, to search for the wisdom inherent in every rock and leaf. I resolve to walk my life in beauty, harmony, and balance, and to end my days in honesty and dignity. Then I bow to Richard, who has just finished his own yoga routine, and to the new day.

Until a few months ago, the next piece of my morning routine would have been to pull on my running togs, snap on Isis' leash, and, with her spinning excited big-dog circles at the front door, set off on our morning run. She'd gallop down the sidewalk with her ground-swallowing stride and me in tow, laughing out loud as my legs churned to keep from becoming airborne, until I could settle her into a more dignified trot.

Last fall, Isis began sleeping later and later, and her running pace dropped to a trot, then a jog, and then an amble. Now she's more interested in breakfast than exercise, and our morning run has shrunk to a dash down the sidewalk to pick up the newspaper. When we return, she is eager for food and then more snoozing.

I once defined myself as a runner: my stamina and distance were my barometers of health. When I had no energy to run, I fretted. For years I ran by myself, relishing the solitude. Then Dida, she of the Shar-Pei wrinkles and unquenchably ebullient personality, followed us home one night in Las Cruces, and I discovered the joy of running with canine companions. They're powerful motivators: their enthusiasm rarely flags, even when mine does. Dida was so determined to run with me every day that she refused to be left at home even on the day she died from the tumor that had gradually closed her throat. Isis is more laid-back: these days she would rather doze in the sun than get out at dawn and pound the pavement.

I miss our runs and those chances to read the news of the weather and the seasons, the sounds of juncos twittering their courting songs in spring and ravens croaking as the stars gutter out in frigid winter dawns, the earthy smell of summer days waking up and the crisp air of frost in fall. I've thought about going for the morning run on my own, but Isis gets anxious when I leave without her. Too, I've discovered—and this surprises me—I no longer have a driving urge to push myself. I'm just as happy taking life more slowly. Maybe I'm learning something.

I TURNED FIFTY RECENTLY, nearly twenty-seven years after being diagnosed with an autoimmune disease whose name experts still cannot agree on. It may be lupus, named for the facial rash that signals flare-ups, and known for its fevers, dragging fatigue, and its degenerative effect on internal organs. Or it may be mixed connective tissue disease, an overlap syndrome melding symptoms of lupus with Sjögren's and the chronic muscle pains of polymyositis. I once hungered for a definitive diagnosis—I think I wanted a label to validate my experience—but these days I don't. What matters most to me is to be able to hear what my body is saying and respond to its changing needs. I am acutely aware that no name will change how I manage my health: I'll continue adapting my life to accommodate the symptoms.

I am also acutely aware that words have great power, and names can be prejudicial. Take disease. Labeling a person "diseased" is akin to giving them stigmata, visible marks of their inability to maintain normal health. That's not helpful with a chronic condition like mine, which defies the ministrations of Western medicine. Thinking of myself as diseased just makes me feel sick. Even the word "illness" is injurious. Own up to having a chronic illness, and listeners withdraw, instinctively pulling away to protect themselves. I'm not contagious.

The story that Western medicine tells about autoimmune diseases stems from World War II–era research that quite naturally—given the events of the time—envisioned the immune system as a military operation with a variety of cells patrolling the body in a sort of biochemical halt-who-goes-there, search-and-destroy scenario. In this tale, autoimmune diseases arise when, for reasons unknown, these defenders go awry and mistake our tissue for foreign invaders. The upshot is an attack from within, causing the symptoms that characterize these conditions.

"Once again, medical language is loaded, this time with military metaphors," writes Terry Tempest Williams in *Refuge*. "Can we be at war with ourselves and still find peace?"

A new model of how the human immune system works, developed by immunologist Polly Matzinger of the National Institutes of Health, could help. Our immune systems, Matzinger believes, protect us not by naively searching for foreign bodies to destroy but by responding to signals of danger broadcast by our cells. Matzinger explains her model with an analogy to her Border collie Annie. When guarding a herd of sheep, Matzinger says, Annie doesn't waste her energy casting about for invaders; instead, she snoozes, one ear cocked to the sheep. When they show signs of unease, she leaps into action. Dendritic cells in our bodies, says Matzinger, act like Border collies. These cells' fingerlike projections touch from fifty to five hundred neighboring cells. As long as this "flock" acts normally, the dendritic cells snooze. As soon as one of the cells does something abnormal, such as spewing its potentially toxic contents after being infected by a virus, or leaking cell fluids after sustaining a physical injury, the dendritic cells leap into action like so many Border collies, triggering the process we call the immune response.

It may seem like splitting hairs to move from seeing the immune system as a search-and-destroy patrol to seeing it as a protective Border collie. But the shift in character between the two stories has profound implications. For one thing, Matzinger's model may fit our experience more closely, explaining many important exceptions the conventional model cannot account for, including why the immune systems of pregnant women do not routinely attack and destroy the "foreign tissue" that makes up normal fetuses. Moreover, her model opens the possibility that the immune systems of people diagnosed with autoimmune diseases aren't turning on us; they are simply responding to danger signals generated by the cells of our connective tissue.

Further, recent studies suggest that the immune system may act more like a cellular trash-hauler and hazardous-materials disposal team, mopping up the molecular debris spilled in the everyday wear and tear of cells, and identifying and hauling away both innocuous but no longer needed compounds and potentially harmful substances and organisms. In addition, new research on chronic fatigue syndrome shows that some of us are genetically and physiologically less able to adapt to certain life stresses.

These stories suggest a fundamental rethinking of the process of autoimmune diseases, emphasizing the role played by chronic cellular damage caused by long-term emotional and physical stress. We already know that stress can damage or kill cells, and stress reduction techniques can result in significant improvement. If those of us diagnosed with autoimmune diseases respond to stressors in a way that is injurious or fatal to specific kinds of cells—for instance, insulin-making cells, the flexible cells deep in our lungs, or the cells that line our joints—the resultant chronic damage would trigger an equally chronic immune response. As our immune systems work to dispose of the stress-damaged cells, we would experience fever and inflammation, joint damage, lung scarring, the inability to process sugars, and the other symptoms we call autoimmune diseases. Perhaps the real story of these conditions is not about disease at all. It may simply rest on individual variations in the body's complicated and tangled response to the factors we call stress.

Whatever the story, I've learned to live within the shifting parameters of my health, and despite my initial prognosis, here I am. Not perhaps as healthy as I might wish to be, but, as Ram Dass emphatically declares in the title of his memoir about life after a near-fatal stroke, very much "still here."

AND HERE IS ISIS, eager for breakfast. The Great Dane who came to us four and a half years ago emaciated and who quickly gained more than fifty pounds may sleep most of the time now, but she has not lost her enthusiasm for food. As her stamina has waned, we've shifted her from premium canine kibble to a more easily digested—and, some might say, even more premium—senior diet of cubed organic chicken breast over brown rice and steamed vegetables, made from scratch each day.

I feed Isis her hot meal of chicken and rice spiked with applesauce for vitamins and yogurt for beneficial microbes, and then Richard and I sit down to our own breakfast. The sun hasn't yet spilled over the ridges of the Arkansas Hills and into our windows, but solar energy stored in the polished concrete floors keeps the place cozy despite the morning's low of nine degrees. While the floors radiate the last of the heat from yesterday's sunlight, the fire in the woodstove adds its warmth from another kind of solar energy stored as tree flesh.

As I stand in the kitchen, steaming milk for my post-breakfast cocoa, I look out the window over the sink at the view down the valley. A murky haze of moisture from last night's snowstorm lingers in the air, tinged pink by the rising sun. Two groups of ducks fly over, wings beating so fast they seem to twinkle, headed downriver. Cars pull into the Safeway parking lot and shoppers hurry into the store, squeezing in an errand on their way to work. A solitary walker passes on the trail across the creek, dog trotting in front.

I take my cocoa to the living room couch, positioned midway between the bank of windows that invite the sun's warmth inside in winter (with overhanging eaves to exclude that same sun in summer) and the woodstove with its dancing flames. I curl up facing the fire and peruse the day's newspaper, beginning with news of the world, working my way to local news and finally the sections on home and entertainment. I note that my horoscope predicts a five-star day of "unusual creativity," and then chuckle through the comics.

By the time I have finished the paper and answered the most urgent e-mail, a category that spans the daily missive from my seventy-six-year-old mother, a question from a grade-school-aged fan, a friend's message, a request for a book-jacket blurb, and a note from a magazine editor, the sun has risen and floods in the windows. Isis' joints creak like mine as she heaves herself to a standing position and then circles on her dog bed before plopping down, her back in the sunlight, with a groan.

WHEN WE BOUGHT THIS half-block of decaying industrial property with Richard's studio and office, plus the gift of our block of creek frontage, we imagined building our house there "someday." It was Richard's dream to build a house with his own hands, using earth-friendly materials wherever possible. Several years later, we and a fair portion of the male inhabitants of our neighborhood spent a hot summer Saturday watching a trackhoe clear our site. The operator carefully combed our weedy ground with the giant teeth of the huge open bucket, wrenching hunks of unidentified industrial junk out of the soil and dropping them into a waiting dump truck. Thereafter, house construction proceeded in fits and starts on the pay-as-you-go plan: whenever we had money and/or Richard had time between consulting jobs, the footers went in, the slab was poured, the walls went up, the roof went on, the wiring threaded through, the insulation was sprayed in, and so on. Neither of us had any idea that the process would lead him to a new path as an abstract sculptor who works in found boulders, steel, and wood, or that construction would take so long. Thirteen days shy of six years from the date our building permit was issued, we moved in.

While Richard built, I worked on landscaping. (My construction talents are limited to design consultation, picking colors, scheduling subcontractors, and paying bills.) Richard's shop sat in one corner of the property, closest to the creek and to the alley that separated the new property from the duplex. The new house butted up against the shop at one end of the longer leg of its lopsided H shape and sprawled from there toward the opposite corner of the property, creating two courtyards and a front yard that faced the end of the block. With average annual precipitation of less than 10 inches, I didn't want a lawn. (I've never had an ambition to learn the rituals of mowing and applying deadly chemicals to my household landscape.) I envisioned a yard that harked back to the native bunchgrass and fringed sage prairie that would have graced our site before the railroad arrived in the 1880s and Salida was born. (Which meant I'd be welcoming back the very same "cactus, sage, and rocks" that Richard's elder siblings spent after-school hours picking out of the yard of their Salida home a few blocks away in 1952 in order to grow a lawn.)

I contacted a local couple who collected and sold native plant seeds and asked if they could come up with a seed mix that might succeed on challenging soil layered with roadbase, fly ash, and other industrial leavings. They looked the place over, shook their heads doubtfully, and returned with bags of what they half-jokingly called roadbase mix. Richard and I seeded an experimental strip at one freshly weeded edge of our windswept site that fall, spread a layer of wood chip mulch to keep the seeds from blowing away over the winter and discourage weed germination, and laid soaker hose so we could water the area in a way that mimicked natural patterns of rain and snowfall.

By the second year, our roadbase mix had sprouted a flourishing strip of perennial wildflowers and grasses, including the brilliant red-orange spikes of Indian paintbrush, which is said to be one of the toughest wildflowers to germinate from seed. None of the baby plants grew more than several inches tall their first year, reflecting the abysmal soil, but they thrived—much to the surprise of our seed-suppliers. The following year, I worked on giving our flat-as-a-table yard some contour. We had a few huge boulders hauled in and placed strategically, and my parents helped us build a sinuous mound between the street-side wing of the house and the sidewalk. Then we seeded the rest of the front and street-side yards with our mix of native grasses and wildflowers.

Our native bunchgrass prairie is a traffic stopper when it blooms, but it has one drawback: it's not as conducive to yard parties as a lawn. We wanted some space for entertainment, so we laid a long, narrow rectangle of crushed gravel in the front yard, a boule court for playing petanque, the French game of bowling on gravel that Richard loves to play. It's the only regulation petanque court in Chaffee County, and perhaps in southern Colorado.

Next I turned my attention to the south-facing, creek side of the house. Outside what would someday be the kitchen door was a left-over from the property's industrial past, a remnant of the cement containment wall that had once surrounded the oil tanks above Joe's shed. The site clearing by trackhoe had removed most of the bench-height wall, leaving a U-shaped piece between fifteen and thirty feet long on a side, with its open end facing the house. That wall would enclose my raised-bed kitchen garden. I imagined filling it with wide gravel paths lined by timber-framed beds the height of the two-foot wall—perfect for sitting on while working the garden, or for guests at our yard parties.

When Richard's helper Ed was between projects, he built the raised beds and filled them with soil mined from a meadow in the mountains. Despite Richard and Ed's conviction that the garden was much too big for our needs, I filled it edge to edge with as-paragus and strawberry plants, three kinds of tomatoes and two of eggplants, mixed lettuces and other greens, along with sugar snap peas, beans, cucumbers, four kinds of summer squash, chard, broccoli, beets, carrots, and herbs. Before we moved into the new house, I faithfully commuted across the alley every day to water my garden and harvest its bounty. Now I simply step out the kitchen door. The garden's fresh produce feeds us from late February, when we begin harvesting spinach overwintered beneath insulating fabric row covers, through early December, when we chop up the last of the windowsill-ripened tomatoes.

Neither the house nor the yard are finished. The private courtyard off our master bedroom and bath needs a deck and landscaping. I'm seeding in more prairie for the area between the petanque court and the kitchen garden. Then there's the courtyard between the garage and Richard's shop, which became a parking lot for materials and equipment during construction, and is now in need of serious attention. Inside, the kitchen cabinets lack doors and drawers; trim, baseboards, and interior doors are still to come. But the house is airy and light, and toasty warm in winter, heated by the sun and the woodstove. It's cool in summer, thanks to overhanging porches and those deep eaves, and to plenty of cross ventilation. Its orientation slightly east of south to catch the low-angle winter sun just happens to coincide with a panoramic view of Salida and the mountains edging the lower half of our valley.

The windows that open the long wall of the wing that is our primary living space to winter sunlight frame the kitchen garden and our wildflower grassland in the foreground, the shrub-lined creek, and downtown Salida. Beyond that to the east the view is of the piñon-pine-dotted ridges of the Arkansas Hills rising across the river; swinging south is the gap where the Arkansas cuts out of the mountains on its way to the distant Great Plains, and across the canyon, the peaks of the Sangre de Cristo Range run west to the Sawatch Range of the Rockies in a wall of snow-splotched mountains.

THAT'S THE WORLD I write about, and the view I see when I carry my laptop into my office and set it on the desk built into a shallow, windowed bay. My eyes range from the kitchen garden in the foreground to the skyline of ridges and peaks. Before I set to work, I turn to the sandstone shelf built into one office wall and greet my totems: the polished black form of Storyteller Turtle by Choctaw artist Randall Chitto, a gift from Richard; the paperweight by a local glass artist with the swirling purple and gold nebula that reminds me of the Milky Way; the round-backed stone bear with the jagged spirit line written in turquoise; the pine-needle basket holding white pebbles that a writer friend picked up from a beach in Greece; the turquoise-studded bird my grandparents brought then-grade-school-age me from Thailand; the leaping dolphin from Mexico; the fossil ammonite; the redwood cones picked up near my mother's childhood home in Berkeley; the tiny jade grizzly Richard brought me from a business trip to Alaska; the brightly painted Norwegian horse; the golden leaves pressed last fall from the cottonwood tree we planted on the creek bank.

Sometime around one o'clock my flow of words peters out for the day. I push myself away from the computer and head for the kitchen. After I prepare Isis' hot meal, I go out the garden door. Here on the south wall of the house, the sun's warmth soaks into my skin, but the air still carries winter's chill. The snow from an unusually plentiful series of weekend storms has nearly melted, and our fall planting of spinach peeks out. The dark green crinkled leaves hug the soil surface, relying on its stored solar heat to stay alive. I pick a handful to augment our lunch and carry them inside to rinse. As we eat our simple meal of salad, bread, and fruit, the taste of that fresh spinach lingers on my tongue. It is our *goût de terroir*, a French term often translated as "taste of earth," which has come to be associated with local and seasonal foods. This taste of our garden-to-come is as local and seasonal as one can get, a connection with the soil right out our kitchen door and the sunlight that nurtures it and us, day after day.

When I talked Richard into the idea of a raised-bed kitchen garden, and into lending Ed to build it, I had no inkling of how much of our food supply it would provide, even in the dead of winter, or of how thoroughly its bounty would root us in this place. Nor did I realize that, nourished only with sunlight and aged manure—

sans pesticides or synthetic fertilizers — it would gift us with such a bounty of produce that we supply family and friends, plus a whole community of other lives.

In summer, there's the broad-tailed hummingbird hovering in a green-backed blur as she sips nectar from the purple flowers of the anise hyssop. The pink spikes of Rocky mountain bee plant that sprouted on their own in the tomato bed and vibrate with native bees: tiny ones barely big enough to see circle the blossoms in a cloud, waiting for their chance to dart around the bomber-sized bodies of yellow-and-black-striped bumblebees and the hovering phalanx of metallic green sweat bees. That bee plant — I think of it as Joe's gift, even though he's long gone now — attracted so many native bees to our garden last summer that our eight tomato plants produced a bumper crop for our short, high-altitude summer of more than one hundred pounds of fruit. (Tomato flowers are self-fertile, but they produce much more fruit when visited by bumblebees. Commercial tomato growers cultivate bumblebee colonies in their greenhouses to increase tomato yields.) A garter snake, consumer of slugs, snails, and other crawling garden grazers, slithers down a knothole in the side of the raised bed to shelter in the shade under the broccoli. Violet-green swallows dip and swoop overhead, snatching flying insects out of the air as butterflies flit through, stopping to sun on the trellis next to the peas. After dark, a bat or two may zip by, hunting the moths whose larvae would otherwise devour our vegetables.

For nearly half the year, we simply step out the back door, pick whatever needs harvesting, and cook with it. We give away bags full of succulent produce to friends, ship boxes to my parents in Denver, and freeze quarts of these fruits of soil and summer sunlight to nourish us through high-country winters. And when the snow melts off the garden on a warm and sunny February afternoon, there are green and crinkly spinach leaves to pick.

AFTER LUNCH, Isis is feeling frisky and so am I. I clip on her leash and off we go, headed for the post office, a few blocks away. She trots along in front of me with head high and yard-long tail gently waving. After a couple of blocks, her gait slows and her back legs begin to drag, her nails scraping on the sidewalk. By the time we turn for home, she is limping with the rolling gait of one who has just returned from weeks at sea. When we reach the house, she collapses on her bed and is soon fast asleep.

I migrate to the couch, stretching out with my feet up on the cushions, and Isis nearby. This is the quiet time I need to let mind and body unwind and recharge my spirit. I look up to the peaks to gauge the weather in the size of the snow plumes billowing off their crests, and chart the progress of the season in the bare ground beginning to emerge on their lower slopes. I watch ravens sail past and wonder when the red-fisted rhubarb buds in the garden and the daffodil leaves just peaking above the soil next to the kitchen door will get the signal to grow and bloom. I am fortunate: even though I no longer have the stamina to spend my days outside, I am not cut off. This house invites the outside in, reminding us that we are part of the community of lives that animates the landscape we share.

After a while I pick up my laptop to answer e-mails and read the news online. When I put the electronic distraction aside, I notice that the slanting late afternoon sunlight accentuates the subtle mottling in our concrete floor, a variation in earthy hues that caused a visiting artist to exclaim, "You've brought the ground inside!" We didn't plan our floor to look this way: we figured we'd tint the bare slab after the walls were in, using a custom compound that would react with the lime in the concrete, coloring it from within. But we didn't like the way the test patch looked, so we dispensed with the expensive stain and simply polished the slab just as construction left it, tinted by the ochre over-spray from the insulation crew with ghostly shadows left by piles of lumber and construction equipment, the stains left after a house finch was trapped inside overnight, the amber splatters where a plumber splashed oil, and here and there, the tactile impressions of leaves that blew in when the slab was poured one blustery late-November day. "You use what you find," a filmmaker I interviewed once said. Looking at our unplanned floor finish, I see what he meant. The sunlight skitters along the serrated edge of one leaf impression, and makes the whole floor come alive, like soil on a spring afternoon.

AS THE SUN SETS behind the peaks to the west, Isis shakes and comes over to nuzzle me. Her baggy eyes and enormous graying muzzle give her a pitiful look that I interpret as a plea for dinner. I pet her and then turn away, but she is insistent.

"Okay, okay!" I get up and go to the kitchen to heat her meal. She pads after me stiffly, even mustering the energy and grace to prance for a minute in the kitchen doorway, drooling as I scoop her food into her bowl.

I pour Richard's favorite beer, a Belgian ale from a nearby micro-brewery, put pretzels into an oiled walnut bowl shaped by my great-uncle from branches pruned out of his orchard, and get myself a glass of filtered water from the tap. Richard comes over to sit in the rocking chair next to me on the couch. We both turn to look at the last light of the sunset before it fades from the highest peaks of the Sangres.

"What thoughts?" I ask.

"Just that I love you."

It's been twenty-four years since that date at the hot springs where the snowflakes sizzled as they hit the steaming water and the stars dazzled as the sky went black. Twenty-four years since our improbable instant pairing. And when we sit together like this at the end of the day and I ask what's happening, what springs to his mind is love.

I don't think I knew what love was back then. Now I believe I do. It's how we are together: the way his face lights up when I walk into a room. His hand, reaching for mine. The fact that our bodies, though altered by the years, still fit like paired puzzle pieces. That we can be comfortable in silence, yet be eager to hear what the other has to say. It's that sitting side by side at the end of a long day, when I ask what he's thinking, he says, "That I love you." And I know he means it.

IN THE SHARP COLD of the darkness before bedtime, Isis and I go for a short walk down the block to jog her bladder into emptying and help ensure that her bed will stay dry through the night. She ambles along with head high and yard-long tail waving, squats with a gush, and then turns to trot back to the warmth of home. I look up at the heavens, checking the stars, but clouds obscure the sky.

In bed later, I lie on my side while Richard stretches next to me, his strong hands massaging the tension from my shoulders and neck. As his fingers tease out my knots, I say aloud my affirmation to live my life alongside his in a way that is nurturing and supportive, that encourages and inspires his creativity, and that will help him follow his dreams and intuitions. He slips under the covers and speaks his own pledge to me. We cuddle close, holding hands. He falls asleep almost immediately. It takes a while for my body to quiet down. I listen to the data from within and without: the rattle of air rushing through my dry sinus passages, the "clunk" as I rearrange my shoulder joint, Isis' wheezing breathing, the whooshing waves of wind pouring down the valley as a weather front passes, the sound of a car going by, and the tick as something in the house framing contracts in the cold. I let the impressions and feelings of the day slide away. And I remind myself of my blessings: I am thankful for the gifts of work that I love, this house and its bountiful garden, the support of friends and family, and my heart's connection to the community of the land. I am thankful for the nose-tickling pungence of big sagebrush, the sound of the creek, Isis' company, the feel of Richard's warm body next to mine, the days I never expected to see. This life, come what may.

JUST BEFORE I DRIFT OFF, I open my eyes once more, reach for my glasses, and look out the skylight that Richard painstakingly fitted into the slanted ceiling high over our bed at just the right place for stargazing. Through a gap in the clouds, I spot Sirius, the Dog Star, twinkling brightly next to the sparkling river of the Milky Way, and just at the edge of the pane, Orion, striding across the heavens. Then the clouds shift, I take off my glasses, and my view dissolves into dreams.

NOTES, INSPIRATION, AND RESOURCES

What follows is an annotated list of books, journal and magazine articles, websites, and other resources I drew on to write this story. These notes refer to quotes or specific research and are listed by the chapter and page where they appear. General information comes from the sources listed by topic in "Other Sources." That section also includes other books and resources I found useful and inspiring.

Page vi: But to look at the stars always makes me dream. . . . Vincent Van Gogh, letter to his brother Theo, July 9, 1888, in *The Complete Letters of Vincent Van Gogh*, 3 vols. (Bullfinch, 2000). [Read this letter online in a lovely presentation with Van Gogh's drawings at http://webexhibits.org/vangogh/letter/18/506.htm.]

CHAPTER ONE

Page 4: I and all the other lives on Earth are connected to the stars. . . . William Bryant Logan, *Dirt: The Ecstatic Skin of the Earth* (Riverhead Books, 1995), pp. 7–9. [A meditation on the most mundane of substances by the writer-in-residence at the Cathedral Church of Saint John the Divine that weaves biology with cosmology to reveal the sacred.]

Page 5: The title stood out in bold type. . . . Norman Cousins, *Anatomy of an Illness as Perceived by the Patient: Reflections on Healing and Regeneration* (Bantam Books, 1981). [This groundbreaking look at medicine and healing from a former editor of *Saturday Review* helped me understand the limitations of Western medicine.]

Pages 8–9: What I learned was as bewildering as it was illuminating. . . . [See the National Institute of Arthritis and Musculoskeletal and Skin Diseases at http://www.niams.nih.gov/hi/index.htm for handbooks on specific autoimmune diseases.

Page 9: "the kingdom of the sick." Susan Sontag, *Illness as Metaphor* (Farrar, Straus, and Giroux, 1977), p. 3. [Sontag's indictment of the damaging affects of our perceptions of illness and the military metaphors used to treat it was written more than three decades ago but is unfortunately still relevant.]

Page 12: I am, as Kurt Vonnegut's Mr. Rosewater described himself, "a very slow realizer." Kurt Vonnegut, *God Bless You, Mr. Rosewater* (Dial Press, 1998; originally published 1965), p. 36.

CHAPTER TWO

Page 22: Neurologist Oliver Sacks tells a story. . . . Oliver Sacks, "Neurology and the Soul," *New York Review of Books*, November 22, 1990, p. 47. [A classic look at the dangers of splitting psyche from soma.]

Page 23: "In ancient cultures. . . ." Jack Kornfield, *A Path with Heart: A Guide through the Perils and Promises of Spiritual Life* (Bantam Books, 1993), p, 83. [Kornfield's writing resounds with spiritual common sense: what we know we know, but often forget.]

Page 31: Researchers studying connective tissue diseases. . . . Damaris Christensen, "Why Does a Woman's Immune System Sometimes Turn on Her?" *Science News*, July 28, 2001, pp. 58–60. [This magazine does a beautiful job of summarizing recent research, including illuminating quotes from the researchers themselves. It is also online at http://www.sciencenews.org.]

Pages 32–34: The "seas" of sagebrush. . . . [There's not much information about sagebrush in popular literature, perhaps because it has long been considered a "weed," not because it is not native but because cows avoid its pungent foliage, a prejudice based on a cow's-eye view of the landscape. This section is distilled from several sources, including Stephen Trimble, *The Sagebrush Ocean: A Natural History of the Great Basin* (University of Nevada Press, 1989; Jack Nisbet, *Singing Grass, Burning Sage* (Graphic Arts Publishing Co., 1999); and my article "The Next Spotted Owl?" *Audubon*, November 2000, pp. 64–71.]

Page 34: "The impulse to *do* when sick is understandable. . . ." Larry Dossey, *Healing Words: The Power of Prayer and the Practice of Medicine* (Harper Collins, 1993), p. 19. [An illuminating look at the role of faith in healing.]

CHAPTER THREE

Page 46: . . . what Aldo Leopold called "the community of the land." Aldo Leopold, *Sand County Almanac*, 2nd ed. (Oxford University Press, 1968), pp. 204–212. [If you want to begin to understand ecology and the interrelationships that sustain life, start with this book.]

Pages 48–49: In the 1640s, a nineteen-year-old English apprentice. . . . George Fox, *The Journal of George Fox* (Friends United Press, 1976), pp. 68–82. Also Hugh Barbour and J. William Frost, *The Quakers* (Friends United Press, 1988).

Page 49: "True silence. . . ." William Penn, from *Fruits of a Father's Love*, quoted in *Quaker Faith and Practice* (Yearly Meeting of the Religious Society of Friends [Quakers] in Britain, 1994).

Page 52: Some of science's greatest leaps. . . . Linda Jean, Shepherd, *Lift-*

ing the Veil: The Feminine Face of Science (Shambala Publications, 1993). [A lucid and eye-opening look at the gender bias in the culture of science.]

Page 55: It is the kind of intense, sustained focus. . . . Evelyn Fox Keller, *A Feeling for the Organism: The Life and Work of Barbara McClintock* (Times Books, 1984). p. 198. [This biography of one of science's most influential thinkers says as much about the culture of science and dissent as it does about McClintock's extraordinary work.]

CHAPTER FOUR

Pages 61–62: Falling in love at first sight. . . . "Cor, You Don't Half Smell," *Economist*, January 24, 2001, p. 80; and Damaris Christensen, "Why Does a Woman's Immune System Sometimes Turn on Her?" [See full citation above, under Chapter Two.]

Page 66: Scientists studying heart and blood vessel disease. . . . Christiane Northrup, *Women's Bodies, Women's Wisdom* (Bantam Books, 1998), pp. 738–739. [Northrup's book demonstrates repeatedly that illness is intimately related to our emotions; her chapters are full of examples of how to heal from within as well as without.]

Page 66: In *Molecules of Emotion*. . . . Candace Pert, *Molecules of Emotion* (Scribner, 1997), pp. 22–24. [The story of Pert's novel work in tracking and understanding the molecules that transmit our feelings from our brains throughout our bodies, and an inside look at the costs of swimming against accepted scientific theory.]

Pages 68–69: Humans are not the only species that pair for life. . . . Bernd Heinrich, *Mind of the Raven* (Harper Collins, 1999). [The information on courting behavior is drawn from Heinrich's immensely readable book and from personal observations.]

Page 72: "We become what we tell ourselves that we are." Mary Pipher, *The Shelter of Each Other* (G. P. Putnam's Sons, 1996), p. 271. [A heartfelt and encouraging look at simple ways to heal and strengthen families.]

CHAPTER FIVE

Page 81: "It's colder than a stepmother's tits out there!" Colleen Mc-Cullough, *The Ladies of Missalonghi* (Avon Books, 1987), p. 24. [This throwaway phrase from an otherwise delightful novel illustrates the pervasiveness of the negative stereotype applied to stepmothers.]

Pages 81–82: Anthropologist Sara Blaffer Hrdy argues. . . . Sarah Blaffer Hrdy, *Mother Nature: A History of Mothers, Infants, and Natural Selection* (Pantheon Books, 1999), p. 57. [Hrdy's theories of the evolution of mothering behavior informed my ideas on step-parenting, even though she doesn't mention stepmothers in the book.]

Page 86: We were unwittingly following in the footsteps. . . . Henry David Thoreau, *Walking* (Cosimo Classics, 2006), p. 6.

Page 87: Biologist E. O. Wilson calls humans' innate empathy. . . . Edward O. Wilson, *In Search of Nature* (Island Press, 1996), p. 165. [Wilson's writing is always thought-provoking. This collection of essays on a variety of topics is a good introduction to Wilson's ideas and work.]

Page 87: This instinctive connection may originate in the molecules. . . . Lynn Margulis and Dorion Sagan, *Microcosmos: Four Billion Years of Microbial Evolution* (Summit Books/Simon and Schuster, 1986), pp. 120–126. [The classic elucidation of our evolution as composite creatures, dependent on the cooperation of legions of much smaller lives that flourish within us—a rewarding and eye-opening read.]

Pages 87–88: The "bacterial nation" that populates our guts. . . . John Travis, "Gut Check: The Bacteria in Your Intestines Are Welcome Guests," *Science News* 163, May 31, 2003, pp. 344–345; and Alexandra Goho, "Our Microbes, Ourselves: How Bacterial Communities in the Body Influence Human Health," *Science News* 171, May 19, 2007, pp. 314–316. [The first is a fascinating look at the microbial ecosystem that lives in our guts; the second shows us as "a composite of different species."]

CHAPTER SIX

Pages 101–102: . . . what evolutionary biologist Richard Dawkins christens "memes". . . . Richard Dawkins, *The Selfish Gene* (Oxford University Press, 2006), pp. 199–201.

Pages 103–104: Dr. William's assignment was broad. . . . Janice Bowers, "William A. Cannon: The Sonoran Desert's First Resident Ecologist," *Madroño* 37, no. 1 (1990): pp. 6–27. [Janice Bowers' careful research and interest in my great-grandfather's work illuminated and brought to life the scientist I never really knew.]

Pages 108–110: My summons began with a badger. [After I wrote "Picking Up Roadkill," I discovered Barry Lopez' beautiful *Apologia* (University of Georgia Press, 1998), with illustrations by Robin Eschner.]

Page 110: "Story is the umbilical cord between the past and the future." Terry Tempest Williams, in a talk at "Writing and the Natural World," Ranchos de Taos, New Mexico, September 1991.

CHAPTER SEVEN

Pages 116–117: Glaucoma can be a sneak thief. . . . [For more information on glaucoma, see the National Eye Institute's website: http://www.nei.nih.gov/glaucoma/.]

Pages 118–119: Birds breathe the air into their bones. Paul R. Ehrlich, David S. Dobkin, and Darryl Wheye, *The Birder's Handbook: A Field Guide to the Natural History of North American Birds* (Fireside/Simon and Schuster, 1988), pp. 507–509. [The meaning of pneumatization and so much more about birds' diverse lives.]

Page 120: Astronomers generally favor the second possibility. . . . [The theoretical conundrum about dark matter is distilled from two online articles: "Dark Matter," NASA's Imagine the Universe, http://imagine.gsfc.nasa.gov/docs/science/know_ l1/dark_matter.html; and Andrew Chaikin's "Dark Matter: Hidden Mass Confounds Science, Inspires Revolutionary Theories," http://www.space.com/scienceastronomy/astronomy/cosmic_darkmatt_020108-1.html.]

Page 123: . . . the ecology of life in what writer Mary Austin calls "the land of little rain." Mary Austin, *The Land of Little Rain* (Penguin Classics, 1997). [A writer who understood and appreciated the desert long before most people did. This edition has a foreword by Terry Tempest Williams.]

Page 124: "For some people," writes Barry Lopez. . . . Barry Lopez, *Arctic Dreams: Imagination and Desire in a Northern Landscape* (Charles Scribner's Sons, 1986). [I first read this quote while browsing in a bookstore on my lunch hour on a gray winter day in the Pacific Northwest when I was particularly homesick. As I stood there in my business suit and high heels, chills slid down my neck and tears filled my eyes.]

Page 124: The word ["homesickness"] itself. . . . Carolyn Servid, *Of Landscape and Longing* (Milkweed Editions, 2000), p. 13. [Why we bond to place, and what those bonds mean to our species.]

Pages 129–130: Each time we draw a breath. . . . Robin Wall Kimmerer, *Gathering Moss: A Natural and Cultural History of Mosses* (Oregon State University Press, 2003), p. 97. [A numinous look at our relationship to other species through the world of mosses, weaving science and spirituality back together.]

CHAPTER EIGHT

Page 137: In his journal, Quaker George Fox recounts. . . . *The Journal of George Fox*, p. 87.

Page 149: That same tension lies at the core of our galaxy. . . . Marc Kaufman, "Massive Black Holes May Also Be Creators," *Denver Post*, November 1, 2007. [This is just one of many recent articles illuminating a whole new understanding of black holes' role as "recyclers" of stellar energy.]

CHAPTER NINE

Page 155: "Once again, medical language is loaded. . . ." Terry Tempest Williams, *Refuge: An Unnatural History of Family and Place* (Vintage Books, 1991), p. 43. [A powerful memoir exploring the death of the author's mother from cancer and the healing power of place.]

Pages 155–156: A new model of how the human immune system works . . . . Mary Anne Dunkin, "Polly's Spin," *Arthritis Today*, March–April 1999, pp. 38–42, 55. Also Polly Matzinger, "The Real Function of the Immune System or Tolerance of the 4 D's," http://cmmg.biosci.wayne.edu/asg/polly.html. [Both pieces introduce Polly Matzinger's revolutionary theory of how the immune system functions, and give glimpses of how this extraordinary thinker arrived at her novel understanding.]

Page 156: . . . new research on chronic fatigue syndrome. . . . Jennifer Corbett Dooren, "Chronic Fatigue Is Linked to Immune System," *Wall Street Journal*, April 25, 2006; and Thomas H. Maugh II, "Fatigue Syndrome Linked to Gene Changes, Study Says," *Denver Post*, April 21, 2006, p. 2A.

Page 163: Tomato flowers are self-fertile. . . . Susan J. Tweit, "Creating Buzz," *Audubon*, May–June 2007.

OTHER SOURCES

Here are other books and websites that have inspired and informed this story. (Those listed in the notes are not repeated here.)

ASTROLOGY AND STAR LORE

Cornelius, Geoffrey, and Paul Devereux. *The Secret Language of the Stars and Planets: A Visual Key to the Heavens*. Chronicle Books, 1996, pp. 76–77. [A well-written guide to the knowledge we have assigned to the heavens over time.]

Fenton, Sasha. *Astrology for Wimps*. Sterling Publishing, 2003. [A serious introduction to astrology that takes itself lightly, with a great sense of humor.]

Miller, Dorcas S. *Stars of the First People: Native American Star Myths and Constellations*. Pruett Publishing, 1997. [This book and the next one listed below are beautiful collections of Native star knowledge.]

Monroe, Jean Guard, and Ray A. Williamson. *They Dance in the Sky: Native American Star Myths*. Houghton Mifflin, 1987. [See notation for the work by Dorcas Miller, above.]

ASTRONOMY

Brunier, Serge. *The Great Atlas of the Stars*. Firefly Books, 2001. [Spectacular photos of the constellations and nebulas by Akira Fujii make this book.]

International Dark-Sky Association. http://www.darksky.org. [A tremendous resource on light pollution issues and ways to return dark skies to your community.]

NightSky. http://www.space.com/nightsky/. [Sponsored by the makers of Starry Night, a computer program for backyard astronomers, this site is a great place to learn about what is happening in the night skies.]

Raymo, Chet. *An Intimate Look at the Night Sky*. Walker and Co., 2001. [One of my favorite guides to the night sky, written by a perceptive thinker in luminous prose.]

Ridpath, Ian, and Wil Tirion. *The Monthly Sky Guide*. Cambridge University Press, 1987. [Dated, but still a great resource.]

Arthritis Today. http://www.arthritis.org/resources/arthritistoday/. [The website of the Arthritis Foundation and its magazine, *Arthritis Today,* is chock-full of information on rheumatoid arthritis and related autoimmune diseases and syndromes, including Raynaud's, Sjögren's, and lupus.]

Lupus: A Patient Care Guide for Nurses and Other Health Professionals. National Institute of Arthritis and Musculoskeletal and Skin Diseases, 2006; available free from http://www.niams.nih.gov. [This is, hands down, the best guide to living with lupus I've found. If you have lupus or any related autoimmune disease, order one of these for yourself and one for your primary health-care provider.]

Mayo Clinic. http://www.mayoclinic.com. [On the website of the Mayo Clinic, you can search for the specific name of autoimmune diseases and retrieve authoritative summaries and information on diagnosis and treatment. Easy to use, comprehensive, and clearly written. For example, see its description of mixed connective tissue disease, which is rare enough that it's hard to find information on: http://www.mayoclinic.com/health/mixed-connective-tissue-disease/DS00675.]

Sjögren's Syndrome Foundation. http://www.sjogrens.org. [This foundation's website is a helpful resource for information on what is often called dry-eye syndrome but affects every mucous membrane in the body.]

COMMUNITY OF THE LAND AND ECOLOGY

Carrighar, Sally. *One Day at Teton Marsh.* Alfred A. Knopf, 1947. [It's old; it's a novel; it anthropomorphizes the animals. But it's still a wonderfully readable introduction to the community of the land and the characters that make it up.]

Cushman, Ruth Carol, and Stephen R. Jones. *The Shortgrass Prairie.* Pruett Publishing, 1988. [This book shows you the prairie as a community of relationships.]

Harris, Mark. *Grave Matters: A Journey Through the Modern Funeral Industry to a Natural Way of Burial.* Scribner, 2007. [An indictment of our death-care industry and an inspiring look at where death fits in our lives.]

Kingsolver, Barbara. *Small Wonders: Essays.* Harper Perennial, 2002. [Smart, passionate, a fabulous writer about science and life who surprises you with her dry humor—Kingsolver is a treasure.]

Lamberton, Ken. *Wilderness and Razor Wire.* Mercury House, 2000. [A painful, honest, and beautiful examination of one life and the impact of nature in prison.]

Lopez, Barry. *Of Wolves and Men*. Rev. ed. Scribner, 2004. [This is the book that started me writing. Not that I blame the author at all.]

Louv, Richard. *Last Child in the Woods: Saving Our Children from Nature-Deficit Disorder*. Algonquin Books, 2005. [A good case for getting kids outside to mess around in nature if we're to survive as a species.]

Moore, Kathleen Dean. *Holdfast: At Home in the Natural World*. Lyons Press, 1999. [Heartrendingly beautiful essays from a philosopher who gets the point of life.]

Pyle, Robert Michael. *Walking the High Ridge: Life as a Field Trip*. Milkweed Editions, 2000. [Pyle's lucid and inspiring meditation on why he studied butterflies and what they have to teach us. Part of the Credo Series edited by Scott Slovic, which includes work by nature writers discussing why they write and live the way they do.]

Russell, Sharman Apt. *Standing in the Light: My Life as a Pantheist*. Perseus Publishing, 2008. [A luminous and beautifully written examination of the belief that the entire universe is holy. Reading it could revolutionize your understanding of religion.]

Terrill, Ceiridwen. *Unnatural Landscapes: Tracking Invasive Species*. University of Arizona Press, 2007. [Read this if you can't imagine what the fuss about invasive weeds is about, or if you just love good writing.]

Watson, Lyall. *Dark Nature: A Natural History of Evil*. Harper Collins, 1995, pp. 212–213. [An examination of the necessity for the dark side of life, and how cooperation benefits life's continuance.]

Zwinger, Ann H. *Beyond the Aspen Grove*. Rev. ed. Johnson Printing, 2002. [Ann Zwinger may not have invented nature writing, but she certainly perfected it.]

GARDENING

Calhoun, Scott. *Chasing Wildflowers*. Rio Nuevo Publishers, 2007. [If you want to understand why some of us grow wildflowers, this book is invaluable.]

Stein, Sara. *Noah's Garden: Restoring the Ecology of Our Own Back Yards*. Houghton Mifflin, 1993. [The subtitle says it all. It's written about the Northeast, but the ideas are inspiring and applicable to yards and gardens anywhere.]

Wann, David. *The Zen of Gardening in the High and Arid West*. Fulcrum Publishing, 2003. [If you garden in the inland West, read this book.]

Dass, Ram. *Still Here: Embracing Aging, Changing, and Dying.* Riverhead Books/Penguin Putnam, 2000. [The straight poop on how to let go and accept what we fear in illness and death.]

Duff, Kat. *The Alchemy of Illness.* Random House, 1993. [Duff's memoir on her experiences with chronic fatigue syndrome will change how you see illness and its role in our lives.]

Hammerschlag, Carl A. *The Dancing Healers.* Harper Collins, 1988. [A physician learns from illness and traditional healers.]

Steingraber, Sandra. *Living Downstream: An Ecologist Looks at Cancer and the Environment.* Addison-Wesley, 1997. [She writes like a poet and researches like a pit bull; you won't emerge from this memoir unaffected.]

QUAKERISM

Barbour, Hugh, and J. William Frost. *The Quakers.* Friends United Press, 1988. [Quaker history, in great detail.]

Pym, Jim. *Listening to the Light: How to Bring Quaker Simplicity and Integrity into Our Lives.* Rider Books, 1999. [What it means—in practical terms—to live a Quakerly life.]

Smith, Robert Lawrence. *A Quaker Book of Wisdom.* William Morrow and Co., 1998. [A charmingly written little book that applies the principles of Quakerism to everyday life.]

Taylor, Thomas, Carol Urner, and Brian Connor. *Cheerfully over the World: A Handbook for Isolated Friends.* Friends World Committee for Consultation. [Although written for Quakers, this booklet is a useful resource for anyone suffering spiritual isolation.]

West, Jessamyn, ed. *The Quaker Reader.* Pendle Hill Publications, 1962. [An anthology of Quaker writings.]

SCIENCE

Bryson, Bill. *A Short History of Everything.* Broadway Books, 2003. [How could anyone resist a book that promises to tell you all the stories of science, with a sense of humor? Don't try.]

Kellert, Stephen R., and Edward O. Wilson, eds. *The Biophilia Hypothesis.* Island Press, 1993. [A collection of writing on Wilson's hypothesis that humans have an ingrained connection to nature. It opens with a beautiful prayer by Abenaki-Czech writer Joseph Bruchac.]

Nabhan, Gary Paul. *Cross-pollination: The Marriage of Science and Poetry.* Milkweed Editions, 2004. [Nabhan nails the relationship between science and art, the heart that science is often missing and the rigor that poetry sometimes lacks. This beautifully, thoughtfully, and passionately written volume should be required reading for everyone, especially scientists and poets.]

Tudge, Colin. *The Variety of Life: A Survey and Celebration of All the Creatures That Have Ever Lived.* Oxford University Press, 2002. [Earth's biodiversity presented in a thorough, lucid, and dazzling survey.]